Praise for *Your Job Survival Guide*

"Gregory Shea and Robert Gunther have written *the* book on how to navigate today's turbulent waters. Full of practical wisdom, research, insight, and humor, *Your Job Survival Guide* shows us how to navigate the whitewater of today's changing business environment while thoroughly enjoying the journey. A great read!"

—Annie McKee, Founder, the Teleos Leadership Institute, and coauthor of the best sellers *Primal Leadership*, *Resonant Leadership*, and most recently, a practical guide to developing and sustaining personal and professional effectiveness, *Becoming a Resonant Leader*

"If gentle currents carried careers in the past, whitewater is the medium today. For navigating the cauldrons of change, Gregory Shea and Robert Gunther draw upon wrenching work moments and rapid river kayaking to draw the map. *Your Job Survival Guide* is an indispensable companion for mastering the turbulence of our era."

—Michael Useem, Professor of Management and Director of the Center for Leadership and Change Management at the Wharton School, and author of *The Go Point: When It's Time to Decide*

"*Your Job Survival Guide* is a provocative book that goes beyond theory. This book is not about avoiding the potholes of organizational life, it's about learning how to step in them and take responsibility for yourself. Shea and Gunther force us to look in the mirror and, in a very practical way, challenge us to behave differently. Quite frankly, the lessons go beyond the perils of our work life; the lessons are useful for day to day living."

—Thomas Saporito, Ph.D., President, RHR International Company

"In today's world there is no such thing as steady state. Greg and Robert have put together a great owner's manual for thriving in a world where change is the constant."

—Michael Rechtiene, President, Animas Corporation, a Johnson & Johnson Co.

"Today's world requires us to continuously reinvent our company by adapting it to the evolving world. At the core of that process lies one's ability to efficiently manage necessary changes. Gregory Shea and Robert Gunther beautifully describe this important challenge and offer simple and concrete solutions to meet them. As head of a company that lives its fundamentals—'people are our main asset'—I am recommending this book to all our executives and managers as a key tool to meet the future."

—Patrick Firmenich, CEO, Firmenich

"It is no secret that continual *change* dominates most business life today. Most thinkers and writers addressing managing, leading, or surviving change, however, tend to focus on examples of one change after another, often complex and multiyear strategic change, but still bounded by the one story. Shea and Gunther take head-on the reality that we actually need to manage and lead in an environment of continuous, ongoing, major change. They then address the role of the protagonist in *many* simultaneous and overlapping change processes, which is the reality today. They offer wonderfully accessible experiential and practical observations and advice for *you*, the actor in these many stories. This is sound, practical, and readily applied advice. And it's also in a form that allows you to 'dip into' the book in different sections and take a few valuable insights to put into practice immediately—a truly wonderful addition to the practitioner's literature on leading change."

—Thomas P. Gerrity, Joseph Aresty Professor of Management, and Dean Emeritus, the Wharton School

"Shea and Gunther's *Your Job Survival Guide* is an easy and important read, overflowing with pragmatic advice about your job in today's white-water world. Using examples ranging from the routine to the spiritual, while sticking close to the metaphor of a memorable journey through turbulent waters, the authors engaged me from start to finish. This book is a great resource both for those individuals stuck in their daily routine as well as organizations who aspire to enhance their work groups."

—Elliot Sussman, M.D., CEO, Lehigh Valley Health Network

"*Your Job Survival Guide* tackles head-on the realities of leadership in the 21st century through the playful lens of the whitewater navigator. The book provides both a comprehensive overview of the challenges that leaders face, but don't always acknowledge, and powerful solutions derived from real life experiences. Accessible and engaging!"

—Meg Jones, Executive VP & Chief Administrative Officer, Children's Hospital of Philadelphia

YOUR

JOB
SURVIVAL
GUIDE

YOUR

JOB
SURVIVAL
GUIDE

A MANUAL FOR THRIVING IN CHANGE

Gregory Shea, Ph.D., and Robert Gunther

Vice President, Publisher: Tim Moore
Associate Publisher and Director of Marketing: Amy Neidlinger
Acquisitions Editor: Jennifer Simon
Editorial Assistant: Pamela Boland
Operations Manager: Gina Kanouse
Digital Marketing Manager: Julie Phifer
Publicity Manager: Laura Czaja
Assistant Marketing Manager: Megan Colvin
Cover Designer: Alan Clements
Managing Editor: Kristy Hart
Project Editor: Chelsey Marti
Copy Editor: Geneil Breeze
Proofreader: Williams Woods Publishing
Indexer: Lisa Stumpf
Compositor: Nonie Ratcliff
Manufacturing Buyer: Dan Uhrig

FT Press offers excellent discounts on this book when ordered in quantity for bulk purchases or special sales. For more information, please contact U.S. Corporate and Government Sales, 1-800-382-3419, corpsales@pearsontechgroup.com. For sales outside the U.S., please contact International Sales at international@pearsoned.com.

This product is printed digitally on demand.

ISBN-10: 0-13-712702-2
ISBN-13: 978-0-13-712702-3

Pearson Education LTD.
Pearson Education Australia PTY, Limited.
Pearson Education Singapore, Pte. Ltd.
Pearson Education North Asia, Ltd.
Pearson Education Canada, Ltd.
Pearson Educatión de Mexico, S.A. de C.V.
Pearson Education—Japan
Pearson Education Malaysia, Pte. Ltd.

Library of Congress Cataloging-in-Publication Data

Shea, Gregory P.
  Your job survival guide : a manual for thriving in change / Gregory P. Shea,
Robert E. Gunther.
     p. cm.
  ISBN 0-13-712702-2 (pbk. : alk. paper) 1. Organizational change. 2. Technological
innovations. I. Gunther, Robert E., 1960- II. Title.
  HD58.8.S4796 2009
  658.4'06--dc22
                              2008010292

*To all who have so generously shared the river with me,
especially my wife, Iris, and our daughters, Emmy and Mer.*
—GPS

*To my father, who taught me to Eskimo roll and gave me a good
line to follow through many a rapid—and to my wife, Cynthia,
and children, Anders, Pelle, and Larkspur,
who have made the journey worthwhile.*
—REG

Contents

Acknowledgments

We thank the many people who have contributed to our thinking, experience, and lives—from the highest levels of corporate leadership to the deepest depths of the Grand Canyon. The journey to this book has taken decades to complete and we had the opportunity to encounter many remarkable people along the way. Too many to name, too important to forget, they made the book possible.

Our sincere thanks to Jennifer Simon for believing in this idea and joining us on this expedition into the heart of permanent whitewater, as well as the wonderful editorial and marketing staff at FT Press.

Thanks to Steve Bowman and Lori Young for their insightful comments on earlier versions and Linda Delbusso for assistance with notes.

We would particularly like to thank our families. They had the harder task, namely to deal with us as we dealt with writing. They supported this work and provided a safe haven when we pulled ourselves, tired and wet, out of the river that was this book. We could not have made this journey without you.

Greg's father passed away as a final version of the book came into view. He, like many members of Greg's family, loved telling and hearing stories. He introduced Greg to a number of those recounted here. He'd have treasured seeing the stories in print in a book written by his son almost as much as his son would have treasured showing them to him.

Finally, our deep thanks to the many executives and managers who have opened their lives and hearts over the years, indeed the decades! Their stories have enriched more than this book. They have enriched the lives of many, including us. They and so many others have looked the turbulence of modern work in the eye day after day, kept paddling, and showed a true line through the rapids. These pioneers point the way for the rest of us.

About the Authors

Gregory Shea, Ph.D., consults, researches, writes, and teaches in the areas of organizational and individual change, leadership, group effectiveness, and conflict resolution. He is President of the consulting firm Shea & Associates; a Principal in The Coxe Group international consultancy; Senior Consultant at the Center for Applied Research; Adjunct Professor of Management at The Wharton School, where he has taught for more than 25 years; an Adjunct Senior Fellow at the Leonard Davis Institute of Health Economics, and a Faculty Associate of the Wharton School's Center for Leadership and Change Management. A Phi Beta Kappa graduate of Harvard, Shea holds an M.Sc. from the London School of Economics and an M.A., M. Phil., and Ph.D. in Administrative Science from Yale. He is a member of the Academy of Management and the American Psychological Association.

Robert Gunther is coauthor or collaborator on more than 20 books, including *The Wealthy 100* and *The Truth About Making Smart Decisions*. He has appeared on CNBC's "Power Lunch," NPR's "Morning Edition," and numerous local and national radio and television programs, and his projects have been featured in *The New York Times*, *Time*, *USA Today*, and *Fortune*. His columns or articles also have been published in *Harvard Business Review*, *American Heritage*, *Investor's Business Daily*, and *The Philadelphia Inquirer*. As founder of Gunther Communications, he has consulted with Fortune 500 companies, universities, and major non-profits. He is a graduate of Princeton University.

PREFACE

We Surely All Will Die

Security is mostly a superstition. It does not exist in nature, nor do the children of men as a whole experience it. Avoiding danger is no safer in the long run than outright exposure. Life is either a daring adventure, or nothing.

—Helen Keller

In 1869, Major John Wesley Powell, a one-armed Civil War veteran and self-made college professor with a passion for exploration, organized a team of nine other men in four boats to tackle one of the last uncharted wildernesses of the United States. They traveled almost 1,000 miles down the Green River and the Colorado River into the heart of the Grand Canyon. In open boats, without life jackets, they made difficult portages around the most dangerous stretches. Sometimes the sheer, towering cliffs prohibited portaging or even scouting. Then, they picked up their paddles, shoved off, and hoped for the best.

This journey proved so harrowing that after two months of battling the river and dwindling rations, three men from the party decided to take their chances overland. At what became known as "Separation Canyon," the men took their leave, saying, "We surely all will die if we continue on this journey." What manager or employee in today's fast-changing organizations hasn't had this same thought? With outsourcing, mergers, reorganizations, and the double-Venti-latte pace of work, the dangers are ever present. Surely, there must be a safer route than remaining on this turbulent whitewater river.

A reasonable person might have agreed with these men who parted company with Powell. Continuing downstream appeared to be certain death. But the men who abandoned the group were killed on their way out. A few days later, Powell and his remaining five crew members made it safely back to civilization, long after the world had given them up for dead. Getting out of whitewater does not necessarily lead to greater security. As Helen Keller said, avoiding danger sometimes is no safer than outright exposure. Sometimes the best path is through the rapids—but you can improve your chances of success with the right skills and equipment.

The two of us, in recent years, separately followed Powell's course down the Colorado River, and each of us benefited from advances in river-running equipment and skills. Greg traveled in a dory designed for this water, with a good life jacket and supporting rafts. Rob paddled a kayak that allowed him to roll (most of the time) when the rapids flipped him. Massive motor launches now cruise like tour buses through the biggest water in the Canyon. In the 80 years after Powell made his journey, a mere 100 people followed his path—and some of them ended up in rough graves along the shores. Today, more than 18,000 visitors per year take this journey.[1] The right skills and equipment make all the difference.

In the same way, ordinary people equipped with the right mindset and skills can successfully navigate the uncommon turbulence of modern organizational life. Living and working in this crazy, rushing world, you might feel at times like the explorers at Separation Canyon. You might be presented with precious few, and decidedly unsavory, options. Proceeding downstream seems to risk disaster, but the route overland, if it even exists, may be no better. As we show in this book, you not only can survive, but you can truly enjoy the journey.

This book started a few years back when Rob attended a session on organizational change that Greg taught at the Wharton School. Greg described this current environment as "permanent whitewater," using a phrase from Peter Vaill.[2] Rob, who has paddled kayaks since he was a teenager and written business books throughout his career, understood what Greg meant by paddling whitewater. It means learning to be comfortable in an environment that scares the hell out of most people. It means developing skills, some counterintuitive ones, such as hanging upside down in your boat while underwater rocks pound on your helmet and your oxygen runs thin. Skills such as the Eskimo roll can convert a nail-biting plunge to oblivion into an exciting adventure.

You need a different way of thinking and acting for this world. First, you need to accept change. Spencer Johnson offered a simple but effective fable about mice and cheese that made this point.[3] But, to accept change is just to start. Today, somebody did not just move the "cheese." The cheese bobs down a river of permanent whitewater; it races over drops and churns through holes. Pity the poor mouse who chases after it—unless, of course, this voyager sits snugly in a kayak, wearing neoprene, a PFD, and a helmet, ready for anything. Once you accept the relentlessness of change—that the cheese keeps moving—you then need to develop the right skills for this new world.

Today, you might feel swept down a rushing, roiling, and seemingly unending river. You are in permanent whitewater. Like Powell, you can't slow or change the pace of this river. But you can change how you look at the river as well as how you react to it. You can pick up your paddle and learn to master the mindset and the skills needed for this turbulent environment, this permanent whitewater world. This book will help you do just that. You hold in your hands a survival guide for your real job: change. But survival is not enough. This book will help you thrive.

Gregory Shea, Ph.D.
Robert Gunther

CHAPTER 1

An Eskimo on the Titanic

The greatest danger in times of turbulence is not the turbulence; it is to act with yesterday's logic.
—Peter Drucker

The *Titanic* was unsinkable. From the captain on the bridge to the humble sailor stoking the fires of the five boilers in the engine room, every crewmember knew that if he just did his job, the future was secure. Then the iceberg happened. On Sunday, April 14, 1912, at 11:45 p.m., the *Titanic* struck a jagged chunk of ice rising 50 to 100 feet above the water. The $7.5 million ship (in 1912 dollars!) broke apart and sank in 2 hours and 40 minutes. No one was secure. Passengers and crew raced to lifeboats or leapt overboard.

When the tragedy struck, the skills and equipment on board were hopelessly mismatched to the challenge at hand. The lifeboats, although exceeding current regulations (which were changed after the disaster), had only enough space for half the passengers and crew. In the chaos, many launched partly filled. The *Titanic's* bountiful amenities—including electric elevators, a swimming pool, a squash court, a Turkish bath, and a gymnasium with a mechanical horse and mechanical camel—were useless in addressing the real challenge that it now faced.[1] (Some might argue that a mechanical camel is pretty much useless no matter what the environment, but we digress.) When the *Titanic* broke apart, the skills valuable on the ocean liner proved of little value in this harshly demanding new environment. What counted were tenacity and skill in battling the elements. The optimism of the "unsinkable" Molly Brown in the face of death became a critical element for survival. (This optimism is vital in an organizational context as well, as we will consider later in the book.) The passengers of the *Titanic* included some of the richest and most prominent people of the age, but their money and power no longer had any meaning. Many counted themselves lucky if they could cling to flotsam in the icy waters. Some 1,500 people died, making it one of the worst maritime disasters in history.

Now, imagine that an Eskimo had been on board the *Titanic*.[2] Perhaps a Polar explorer had brought him to Europe and now planned to have him join a presentation in New York. The Eskimo would have felt ill at ease and sorely out of place in the *Titanic's* elegant dining room. He would have much preferred seal steak in the familiar comfort of his own igloo to the fine china, chandeliers, and cigars. He lacked the skills to prosper on an ocean liner.

But when the ship hit the iceberg, he would have known just what to do. As the ship began to sink, he would have donned his animal skins and walked calmly to his kayak (he certainly wouldn't have taken to the open seas without it). He would have climbed in, fastened on his spray skirt, and launched into the rising waters. He could have paddled through the hallways of the ship, if necessary, out into the open sea. Or he could have "seal launched" off the end of the now-vertical deck of the ship. When waves hit his craft, he would brace and turn with his double-bladed paddle to meet them. If one happened to knock him over, he would have rolled back up.

The Eskimo would have easily made it through the several hours until rescuers came. He had often hunted for longer periods. Or perhaps, tired of the company of his so-called civilized companions, he might have just paddled off in search of land—or another iceberg on which to rest. Unlike the other passengers, he would have had the right tools, skills, and mindset for this environment. And that would have made all the difference.

The environment in which you live and work has changed. You might feel like a passenger on the *Titanic*, plunged into the cold water of a turbulent world. You may find yourself racing downstream on a whitewater river. Do you have your kayak ready?

DANGEROUS WATERS

A talented executive from a major corporation once attended one of Greg's executive education programs. He was about 50, a bit disheveled and wearing a very nice suit, probably an Armani, that set him back at least $2,500. Over the previous decade or so, the *Wall Street Journal* had chronicled his successes in leading high-profile deals.

> The pace of permanent whitewater is relentless. Change happens faster and more dramatically. To stand still is to fall behind.

He kept ducking out of the classroom. At one of the breaks, he apologized for the interruptions, explaining that he faced a difficult decision about returning to work. Six months earlier, he had awoken one morning and found that he just couldn't go to work. He literally couldn't even get himself out of bed. He just couldn't. It shocked him because he loved his work, but he arranged for a six-month sabbatical. He had never done anything like this. Now, at the end of the sabbatical, he had to decide whether to return to his job. He darted from the classroom to his cell phone to talk with senior members of his organization about his future plans.

He realized that he just couldn't go back to work. He didn't know what else to do, but he knew that he couldn't return. He wanted to get back into the river, but he couldn't. He had burned out; his insides had turned to ash. He had pounded through these frothing rapids for too long. He had toughed it out like a warrior, but he hadn't protected and paced himself. Now, he was tired and drenched to the skin, suffering from hypothermia. The steady passage of the river eventually wears down even rock.

The pace of permanent whitewater is relentless. Globalization has redrawn borders, shifted jobs, and created new competitors. Capital moves around the world at the click of a mouse. Technologies change overnight. Telephone companies compete with cable. A computer company, Apple, dominates the music business. Biotech, nanotech, and genomics all appear on the horizon ahead of torrents of change. E-mail, cell phones, and instant messages speed communication and increase the pace. Change happens faster and more dramatically. To stand still is to fall behind.

These forces have shaken up our organizations. Organizations rise and fall amidst ever-mounting competitive opportunities and threats. Mergers and acquisitions dismantle and reconfigure small and large enterprises. These tremors plunge employees into what is politely called downsizing, outsourcing, off-shoring, and rightsizing. Today, such organizational change is as certain as the rising and setting of the sun.

To keep doing the same thing in this environment of change is a recipe for ending up battered or burnt-out, like the executive in Greg's program. You can't brute force your way through permanent whitewater, anymore than you can survive the *Titanic* by being a strong swimmer. You need to recognize that the skills that worked in a more stable environment no longer work in a world of relentless turbulence. The job that you did on the ocean liner is not the job you need to do in permanent whitewater. Like the Eskimo on the *Titanic*, when the iceberg hits, you need to have your kayak ready so you can paddle away from the wreckage and maintain your balance in a sea of unpredictability and turbulence. When the world is turned on its head, you need to learn to think upside down (see sidebar "Thinking Upside Down").

 THINKING UPSIDE DOWN

In kayaking, to learn the Eskimo roll (a maneuver to bring the boat upright after it is flipped over), you have to first become comfortable hanging upside down in the boat, underwater. This violates every human instinct of survival for a creature used to a steady flow of air. Hanging with your head underwater, your first instinct is to get out of the boat and get to the surface as quickly as possible. Learn to suppress your impulse for panic. You need to develop new instincts to get comfortable being uncomfortable.

Wet? Get used to it. Cold? Put on the right gear. Oxygen deprived? Remember you will be better off hanging in for a little longer than taking a long, cold, possibly dangerous swim if you have to bail out of your boat. Everything about your above-the-water existence is reversed underwater. Up is down and down is up.

How do you make this shift? Practice, practice, practice. You first need to practice getting out of the boat, a wet exit. Simple enough, but reassuring to know that you can if you have to. Then you need to practice thinking upside down, and rolling up again. Once you have mastered this in the relative comfort of a swimming pool, you try it in moving water with turbulence all about you.

Then, you are prepared for real water. Here, you are upside down. You are pulled over rocks, pounding on your helmet. You are spun around. It is dark, cold, and wet, but you have trained yourself for this very moment. You can think upside down. You remain calm. You wait for the right moment, and roll up again into the sweet air.

In organizations, you need to change your mindset about what it means to succeed and how to succeed. To build a secure career, you need to take risks. To succeed, you may need to fail along the way. You need to grow comfortable with uncertainty and change. To keep your head above water, you sometimes need to think upside down.

SAILORS AND PADDLERS: YOUR REAL JOB IS CHANGE

Are you prepared when the ship of commerce on which you've staked so much capsizes?[3] At this point, it doesn't matter what you were hired to do, you have one real job: change. How can you do this job well? Transitioning from being a sailor to a kayaker flips many assumptions and beliefs upside down. The attitudes, reflexes, mindsets, and skills are fundamentally different. You need a new mindset and a new set of skills, as we will discuss in the following chapters (summarized in Table 1.1). Instead of running flat out to the next stretch of relatively quiet water, you need to pace yourself. Instead of avoiding failure, you need to embrace failure and prepare to recover quickly. It is not relentless sacrifice, but

> You live and work in a different world. You need new thinking and new skills to succeed. Are you a sailor or a paddler?

optimism and play that keep you afloat and turn bewildering turmoil into exciting adventure. Instead of following orders from the bridge, you need to set your own course—because no matter what the guide books say, you never paddle the same river twice; the flow, the bottom, or the obstacles have changed since the last trip. Instead of finding security in structure, concentrate on building maneuverability and networks to ensure your own "personal flotation." In an environment filled with noise, actions speak louder than words. Instead of staking out a fixed position on the organizational chart, you need skills in designing and participating on ad hoc teams. And you need a certain kind of leadership, and followership, to succeed. You live and work in a different world. You need new thinking and new skills to succeed.

TABLE 1.1 Sailor or Paddler?

Sailor	Kayaker
The world provides a sane pace...usually.	*Pace yourself to preserve your sanity.*
The organization sets the pace, with sailors taking watches. The captain may call "all hands on deck" for limited emergencies, but there is time for recovery afterward. The organization buffers you from the turbulence of the world.	The action does not stop, so you need to set your own pace to avoid burnout and exhaustion. You need to conserve resources in an uncontrollable, rapidly moving, and unpredictable environment. By controlling your pace, you can be in the turbulence but not of the turbulence.

TABLE 1.1 Sailor or Paddler? *(continued)*

Sailor	Kayaker
Avoid failure at all costs. Failure is a disaster to be avoided. Capsizing ends the journey and leads to loss of command. Failure is not an option.	*Prepare to fail gracefully and recover quickly.* Failure, or flipping the boat, is expected, so you need to accept failure and have the right skills and equipment to recover quickly. In fact, taking risks and occasionally failing prove crucial to success. Failure may be the only option.
Work is deadly serious. Keep your nose to the grindstone, work hard, and you will rise up through the ranks. Reserve play for vacations and weekends. Uncertainty and turbulence are a source of danger and fear, to be avoided and controlled if at all possible.	*Paddle hard, play hard.* You will work harder and have more fun in the process. Seek out the play spots. Optimism and resilience are crucial to recognizing the opportunities for fun and renewal. Uncertainty and turbulence provide adventure and play.
The ship provides security. The ship is the source of security, so stay with the ship, no matter what storms and turbulence you meet. The ship will keep you secure as long as everyone does his or her part.	*You are responsible for your own security.* In a turbulent environment, you are responsible for the skills and networks that build your own security. Others may help, but you need your own flotation and you need to know how to self-rescue.
Steady as she goes. The captain and navigator in the map room set the course and the rest of the organization keeps the ship moving toward the coordinates from the top. You know your part and you play it. Stay the course.	*Scout the river to set your own course.* You are responsible for understanding where you are on the river. You need to scout the river and to learn from others. Furthermore, when you hear the roar of the waterfalls—threats to your sanity or health—you need to know when to portage.

TABLE 1.1 Sailor or Paddler? *(continued)*

Sailor	Kayaker
Communicate through the chain of command. The captain issues clear and direct orders that are relayed from the top down through an organization with a common culture, training, and language. Myths and stories often distract you from the job at hand.	*Communicate through symbols, actions, and myths.* In a noisy environment, words lose their meaning, so actions and symbols speak louder than words. Myths make sense of the turbulence and inspire paddlers to carry on.
Know your place and do your job. Every member has a specific and fairly fixed role. A clear hierarchy and chain of command ensures order. It's football—a stable configuration of preset scripts and plays.	*Team for today's run.* Paddlers form ad hoc teams for the day's run. They adjust as circumstances demand. The constant and shared job is change, so roles are reconfigured on-the-fly. It's pick-up baseball—with soccer on demand.
Lead through command and control. Leadership authority comes more from position, and every sailor knows his place. Not following orders constitutes insubordination.	*Lead through trust and personal power.* Leadership derives more from personal power, and roles can shift rapidly. Leaders need to take special care in building trust and selecting their teams. Followers play an active, powerful role and may have to step up to leadership.

THE LIMITS OF FLAT-WATER THINKING

Throughout this book, we use a metaphor of "permanent whitewater." This is more than a literary device. Metaphors play an important role in framing how you think about the world. The wrong metaphors can limit your opportunities and actions. For years, European mariners watched ships disappear over the horizon and concluded that the world was flat. They knew Euclidean geometry. They could see the curved horizon. Intellectually, they had both the theory and the data at their disposal. They should have recognized the roundness of the world. It should have been self-evident. But the flat world blinded them.

> "Flat-water" thinking can blind you to the realities and possibilities of this environment.

So can "flat-water" thinking in a world of permanent whitewater. You have probably received training, explicitly or implicitly, to think and act as a sailor on a stable sea. Just do your job. Move up the ladder. Build your pension. Follow the orders from the bridge, and you will have security. To do so is to think like a sailor on an ocean liner.

But if you have hit the iceberg or are already in whitewater, then you need to change the way you think about your work and your life. The equipment and strategies that you need to address change in permanent whitewater differ fundamentally from those needed on the open seas. In our companies and business schools, we have accumulated tremendous wisdom about how to run ocean liners and navigate through open water. These are important skills, but not the ones that will take you through whitewater. Whitewater requires new perspectives and new skills—for success, and often survival.

Now, more than ever, your success or failure, your destiny, lies squarely in your own hands. This part of a permanent whitewater environment may most excite and, perhaps, most terrify. If you understand the dynamics of whitewater, how to read and run the river, you can become more comfortable with change and can better pace yourself not just for survival but for thriving in the midst of change. On the following pages, we'll explore the distinctive skills, equipment, and mindset you'll need to succeed. Take a firm grip on your paddle and remember: Your success depends heavily on you and your individual skills—skills not only in the job you were hired to do but in your real job—which is change.

 THE TAKEOUT

If you are in permanent whitewater, you need to stop playing the part of a sailor and start thinking and acting like a kayaker. Your job is not your role or your title. Your real job is change.

CHAPTER 2

Working the Eddies
Pace Yourself to Preserve Your Sanity

Row, brothers, row, the stream runs fast,
The rapids are near, and the daylight's past.
—Thomas Moore

The new CFO of the European division of a large, U.S.-based multinational company understood and savored the fact that he had taken on a uniquely challenging job. The senior corporate leadership wanted to transform the division's financial operations from "just" pure finance and accounting to provide in-house consulting to field operations. He and his people would not confine themselves to keeping score. They would also help field executives improve their scores through better understanding of financials and their drivers. The CFO and his staff would help the field executives improve their financial game. His group was to provide coaching to operations staff in the field, especially to those parts of the division that struggled. He knew that this work would require considerable time—to develop new consultative and teaching skills, to travel, and to develop broader working relationships with the field. He knew that he and his people would also need to address the introduction of the euro, the evolving EEU, and the rapids of increasing globalization. All this, and continue to do their day job of managing regional finances.

The company gave him many jobs, but he didn't let them distract him from what he believed to be his true job, namely, change. He knew the internal and external changes could swamp his organization. He knew he needed to find a way to reduce the flow. His group spent considerable time every month collecting data for monthly reports sent to senior corporate managers in New York—this seemed a likely target for simplification. He asked his staff how many data points they collected regularly. They reported approximately 3,600. Next, he asked his staff for the bare minimum number of data points that they felt were needed to fulfill their professional obligations. Just 600. Time gained: 40 to 60 percent (not more, because of the lack of numerical redundancy and the accompanying need for special care and extra checking of the 600 numbers).

The CFO then flew to corporate headquarters in New York City. He proposed to senior management that they narrow the 3,600 data points by a sixth, to 600 measures. This would cut staff time and free them up to tackle their pressing challenges of change, both at hand and down river.

The CFO made a compelling argument to senior executives. He pointed out the folly of trying to do everything. They would burn out staff and erode their ability to deliver on their key transformation initiatives. But the senior managers told him that *he* didn't understand: They wanted their numbers…all of them…*and* they wanted their change, "son." The CFO continued his negotiations over the next three days. Power breakfasts, power lunches, power cocktails, power dinners, power post-dinner drinks. He drew on his reputation. He worked Manhattan's corridors of plate glass and stainless steel as well as he could. In the end, the corporate powers still wanted their numbers, "son." All of them. And they wanted their change.

The CFO considered resigning. He firmly believed that continuing on the ordered route would drown his people. He could see the loss of staff, failure of the change initiatives, and burnout.

Between this rock and a hard place, he made what might be considered a courageous decision—or a very foolish one. He went back to his staff and told them they needed to come up with algorithms to generate the 3,600 points of data from 600 core data streams. They needed to do it with a maximum of 1 percent variation whenever he chose to test them: historically, currently, or in the future. Using these algorithms, they would only have to collect 600 data points but could report all 3,600 to the CEO. The staff developed the algorithms in two weeks, and they worked well. (Note that he was not "cooking the books," just coming up with a complete set of reliable numbers by a more efficient method. This also took place before Sarbanes-Oxley.) Extreme conditions, he believed, sometimes call for extreme measures.

The CFO then met with his 14 direct reports and told them to use these algorithms to complete corporate reports from that day forward. He requested that they not volunteer information about the new approach, but, if asked, they should answer truthfully. He wrote a memo outlining the way to complete the reports henceforth, signed his name, and publicly gave a copy to each of his direct reports. He provided them cover even as he put himself into their hands. Any member of his staff with an ax to grind could have gone to a fax machine, dialed corporate finance, and taken him out right then and there. None of them did. They appreciated that he had their backs in managing the amount of change on their plates...and that they, as they showed, had his.

He bet that handling change well over time mattered most. He bet that the algorithms would buy him and his people enough time (six months he figured) to make enough progress on the change that corporate would forgive his trespass. He also bet that to try to do it all would mean failure. He bet that he could pick the 20 percent of his job that mattered most, which would account for 80 percent of his success. He placed a big professional (and personal) wager, but to do nothing was to bet that he could continue to do everything even as the pace and volume of change in his environment increased. That was a fool's errand, he decided, and too dangerous for his direct reports.

The new method generated no questions from anyone in the organization. Perhaps no one noticed. Perhaps no one cared. What corporate leadership did apparently notice and care about was that the crucial organizational change went well. The CFO successfully transformed his operation without the ill will and employee attrition that too often accompany such initiatives. Furthermore, he saved the energies of his people for the ongoing challenge of conducting business in a changing Europe.

Did the CFO do the right thing in this act of "mutiny"? He circumvented a direct order from senior corporate executives. If you think his job is to obey orders, he obviously did the wrong thing. And if you think his job is to keep track of numbers in the same way it has been done in the past, he was clearly in the wrong. This is the kind of action that might have been in his job description. But if you think that his real job is *change*, then he proved himself to be a superior leader, perhaps even better than his organizational superiors. He recognized the limits of his own resources and those of his staff. He recognized that the danger of bending the rules came to less than the danger of burning out himself and his staff. He did what it took to get the job done, the job of change.

This CFO also saw that he no longer travelled aboard an ocean liner, where the orders of the captain could be cheerfully relayed to the engine room and carried out. On an ocean liner, his actions were clearly mutinous. But they were not on a ship on the open seas. They were paddling together in whitewater. He had to keep his team afloat and keep them from exhaustion. That was the highest priority, because if the whole operation went under or he began losing people along the way, they wouldn't achieve any of their goals or survive the rapids they were sure to meet downstream.

This is not to advocate breaking rules, and certainly not breaking laws. Every manager needs to decide where to draw this line. But you cannot act like a sailor. You cannot blindly follow orders or do your job as it is written in your job description. Besides the moral risks, you might simply perform the wrong job. Updating your job description might occur once a year, but your job (and the challenges it presents) will change much more quickly. If the organization is gasping for air or flying over a waterfall, it won't make much difference that you were just following orders. It is not your real job to follow orders. Your real job is change.

> ## He bet that handling change well over time mattered most.

ALL HANDS ON DECK

The ocean liner organization sets its pace by controlling its passage through the environment. Except for emergencies, employees take turns in clearly defined watches. In contrast, the always-on, 25/8 environment of whitewater has no natural breaks in the action. Unless you control your own pace, you will be swept headlong downstream, battered, bruised, and burnt-out. You cannot control the relentless pace of the environment around you, but you can control your passage through it by learning the skills of effective pacing. You can be *in* the turbulence but not *of* the turbulence.

Kayakers work the eddies behind rocks to move slowly down a fast-flowing stream (see sidebar "Working the Eddies"), standing still while the river rushes past. The CFO did the same thing. He couldn't slow down the world around him, but he could set his own pace moving through the turbulence. He realized he was no longer in a world in which you could rally followers for an exhausting push through perilous waters and then rest and lick your wounds. There is no bottom. Change follows change, relentlessly. He needed to pace himself and his team. He understood that in whitewater environments, you need to learn to pace yourself, and pace your people.

> In whitewater environments, you need to learn to pace yourself, and pace your people.

 WORKING THE EDDIES

Kayakers can control their movement downstream by moving in and out of "eddies," the quiet or upstream-flowing areas behind large rocks or other obstructions. As the river flows past these obstacles, it creates a current that moves in the opposite direction of the main current. A novice might be swept straight through the section of river, but a more experience kayaker will move from eddy to eddy, making slow and measured progress though a very rapidly moving environment. This use of eddies allows paddlers to rest, and to scout the area ahead for obstacles and places to play.

Paddlers can control their movement downstream, even though the stream itself may be uncontrolled. The trick is to recognize that a rapidly moving environment creates these quiet spots—you must know to look and where to look for them. You must also know the wisdom in putting them to good use. Enforce weekends and vacations, even one day.

Take your lunch. Negotiate schedules. It will be more efficient in the long run than rushing pell-mell downstream into who-knows-what. Paddlers develop skills in eddy turns and peel outs to navigate between the eddies and fast-moving currents beyond the eddy line without capsizing. Similarly, we can find ways in organizations, such as the "not to do list," that create these quiet spots and breathers, allowing us to control our pace through a racing, uncontrollable environment.

WE ARE DROWNING IN CHANGE

Demands swirl. They collide against the constraints of time and energy—yours and others'. The list of "to do's" can grow forever as realities change, intermingle, and change again. Sylvia Hewlett and Carolyn Luce discuss the "dangerous allure of the 70-hour workweek." They describe the rise of so called "extreme jobs" with unpredictable workflows, 24/7 client access, heavy responsibility, and travel. Their survey found that 69 percent of 25- to 34-year-olds in these jobs felt they would have better health if they worked less, and 65 percent said they would turn down a promotion if it involved more work.[1]

Many of us are sleep deprived. We operate at the edge of exhaustion. Doctors recommend that adults get 7 to 8 hours of sleep per night. Are you getting that much? The National Sleep Foundation found that less than a third of us are getting 8 or more hours of sleep on weeknights (as shown in Table 2.1). A study of lunchtime in America found that 55 percent of employees took lunch breaks for less than 15 minutes, 63 percent skip lunch at least once a week, and 39 percent took no true break at all. The fact that the researchers even considered a span of under 15 minutes as a "break" is telling in and of itself. This is no way to run a river, a railroad, an army, or anything for very long—much less our own lives.

TABLE 2.1 Weekday Sleep Hours

Fewer than 6	15%
6-6.9 hours	24%
7-7.9 hours	29%
8 or more	30%

National Sleep Foundation's 2002 Sleep in America poll

Those Starbucks cafes on every corner with high-octane beverages provide just one of many signs of the ways this business environment is taking its toll. Caffeine is now the second-largest commodity by dollar volume after oil. America really does run on Dunkin'. (And we worry about our dependence on foreign oil! Perhaps we should be less concerned about OPEC and more concerned about Juan Valdez.) We push for higher and higher levels of caffeine to get the jolt that we need to keep up the relentless pace we think we need (see Table 2.2).

TABLE 2.2 Caffeinated Competition (16 oz.)

Common Joe (8 oz.)	100 mg
McDonald's	148 mg
Dunkin' Donuts	211 mg
La Colombe	241 mg
Wawa	251 mg
Illy	265 mg
Starbucks	322 mg

Philadelphia Inquirer, p. F3, 12/2/04

Caffeine is not the only drug we use to prop open our tired eyes and fill the gaps in our physical and emotional resources. We have taken to using more serious drugs such as amphetamines to keep going. All this works for a while, but at the end of this crazy road is burnout. Between 2004 and 2005, the percentage of people who arrived in ERs with symptoms such as confusion and convulsions from nonmedical use of stimulants rose by more than 33 percent.

For years now, we have asked participants in executive education programs how many have experienced at least one of the following four events in the last year:

- Same staff but at least 10 percent more work without any increase in compensation
- At least 10 percent less staff and no diminution in workload without any increase in compensation
- Responsibility for an additional geographic area without any increase in compensation
- Responsibility for an additional functional area without any increase in compensation

Regardless of industry, 50 to 75 percent of the hands go up. When asked who has experienced two or more of these events, more than 33 percent raise their hands, and there are nearly always at least a few people who have experienced three or four. Ask yourself the same questions. How has the pace of your own company and industry increased over recent years? Do you have any reason to believe that the pace will not continue to quicken? Have you adjusted your own pace in response?

> **Many of us are sleep deprived. We operate at the edge of exhaustion. Doctors recommend that adults get 7 to 8 hours of sleep per night. Are you getting that much?**

The Impact of Exhaustion

A few extra hours with your head off the pillow may seem like a small price to pay for increased success. The price is higher than we think...and the price may, over the long run, actually hinder securing whatever we prize. We suffer and our organizations suffer from fatigue. Fatigue significantly impairs performance. Wakefulness for more than 24 hours impairs performance as much as a blood alcohol level of 0.1 percent. After a day of reduced sleep, we become slightly impaired (as shown in Figure 2.1). By the sixth day, we suffer from noticeable reduced alertness and head toward being dangerously drowsy.

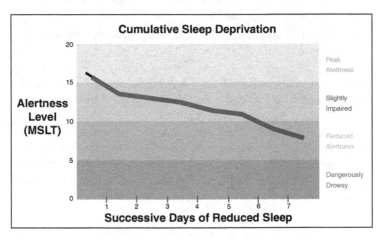

FIGURE 2.1   The cumulative effects of sleep deprivation

Sleep deficits can prove cataclysmic. The total cost of lost sleep to the U.S. economy runs at $45 billion per year, including lost productivity, health care expenses, and motor-vehicle accidents.[2] There are, very likely, much higher indirect costs. The National Highway Traffic Safety Administration attributes more than 100,000 crashes, 71,000 injuries, 1,500 fatalities, and $12.5 billion per year to driver fatigue alone.[3]

Many high-profile disasters have fatigue and sleep deprivation at their center; so do many less visible corporate meltdowns. In *The Twenty-Four-Hour Society*, Martin Moore-Ede attributes the Three Mile Island, Bhopal, Chernobyl, Exxon *Valdez*, and *Challenger* disasters at least in part to human fatigue and "a fundamental conflict between the demands of our man-made civilization and the very design of the human brain and body." Concisely stated, we "were designed to hunt by day, sleep at night, and never travel more than a few dozen miles from sunrise to sunset."[4] Automation has increased productivity so that the same work requires fewer human hours, but we struggle mightily to keep ourselves up to the tasks before us, indeed, to honor our biological limits as well as our organizational responsibilities and technological possibilities.[5]

Individuals and organizations alike make choices about how to handle sleep deprivation. Take the example of the sleepy physician. A physician in a Boston area hospital fell asleep while driving home from an extended shift. Her car struck a pole. She was relatively unscathed, but the hospital decided it needed a new policy to prevent such accidents by weary doctors. So, they came up with a fix—not a solution, just a fix: Instead of ensuring that their physicians had more sleep, the hospital decided to offer tired medical staff vouchers for taxi rides home! This solution amounts to the perfect Band-Aid (pun intended). It addresses the symptom of sleepy drivers, but does nothing to address the underlying cause. Patients, of course, might be more concerned about the impact of weariness on medical practice than on driving. How long before falling asleep at the wheel (or in the back of a cab) might a physician have prescribed potentially lethal medications, determined a course of treatment for an acutely ill patient, or had his or her hands inside a patient's chest cavity?

In fact, physicians who worked one to four marathon sessions (longer than 24 hours) in a given month were 3.5 times more likely to make fatigue-related errors. Those who work five or more marathon sessions are 7.5 times more likely to make fatigue-related errors and three times more likely to make *fatal* errors than when they did not work marathon shifts.[6]

Others besides patients suffer ill effects from sleep deprivation. The situation is unhealthy for the person missing the rest and rejuvenation. Lack of sleep contributes to diseases and obesity. Death from all causes is significantly lower for adults sleeping 7 to 8 hours per night. A study reported in *Harvard Men's Health Watch* concluded that: "Over nine years, men who took vacations were 29 percent less likely to be diagnosed with heart disease and 17 percent less likely to die than those who did not take regular vacations."[7] Exhaustion can kill.

The cycle grows vicious. You fall further behind; you skip vacations and work through weekends. You consume more caffeine. You multitask, dropping another 25 to 50 percent in performance.[8] You are less efficient and make more mistakes, so you work even longer hours, sleeping still less. Your key relationships at work and at home strain under the grind of the sand of unaddressed issues and unresolved struggles. Your pile of work deepens every day. You are drowning in it. Literally, drowning in it.

> "Men who took vacations were 29 percent less likely to be diagnosed with heart disease and 17 percent less likely to die than those who did not take regular vacations."[7] Exhaustion can kill.

STRATEGIES FOR PACING

Every day, new requests came in to the chief information officer of a health care company. The U.S. health care industry was in turmoil. Technology was in flux. Managers of the company's business units who streamed into his office needed new systems, software, or upgrades, constantly—and they needed them now. The CIO knew that this type of relentless pace often leads organizations to swamp and drown their people, creating high rates of turnover and burnout.

He addressed this challenge by developing a strategy to manage the pace of his work using internal contracts. When a new request came in, he would only take it on if other assignments were completed or removed. How did he get away with this? He had an unassailable track record. He was almost always on time and on budget, and often early and under budget. Performance gave him a large store of credibility. He also benchmarked at least every three years so he could demonstrate that his department fell in the top 10 percent of IS departments in the nation. This helped him repel attempts to overwork his people. He found a way to govern pace in an otherwise unpaced industry.

But one Monday morning, his boss put this system to its greatest test. The CEO called him in and dropped a major project on him. The CIO began pulling out his folder of contracts, but the CEO stopped him. "I know about the folder," he said. "Great tactic and it usually works, but it won't work today. No contracts. No folder. I need to get this done in six weeks." No fool, the CIO put away his folder and began to take notes. He would need five people on this project for six weeks, and even at that, this would prove difficult.

That afternoon, he assembled a team and told them about the project. "We've got a big one here. From the CEO. It's a must-do job." Given the urgency, his next words were surprising. He then told the team that they would not start on the project until the following Monday at 7 a.m., a week later. "In the meantime," he said, "today, tomorrow, and Wednesday, I want you to clean off your desks. Delegate, postpone, or cancel. You know I *hate* to break a contract or a commitment, but we have no choice here. If you need any help from me to do any of that, let me know. End of day Wednesday, I want everything off your desk, and I want you gone."

What he said next was even more surprising. "Thursday and Friday, you are on vacation. Free. It'll come out of my account, no PTO charge to you. Also, no e-mails, no phone calls, no pagers. Go home. Rest up and enjoy yourself. Starting Monday at 7, your life will be this project. I'm not even going to tell you what it is until then because you are so conscientious that you'd spend Thursday, Friday, Saturday, and Sunday working on it. I don't want you to. I want you rested on Monday."

This unconventional approach to starting an urgent major project for the CEO got the team's attention. No one missed the symbolic importance of his breaking from his normal "no cancellation" rule, and nobody missed the symbolic importance of free days off up front. The CIO knew that the staff would be working flat out on the project for weeks on end. He also knew that he could not guarantee them a break at the end of the project. Some new project might be dropped in at that point. He could control the front end of this journey, so he carved out time for them to rest up before heading downstream. He rewarded them up front as an act of faith and trust. He did *not* need to elaborate.

In the process, however, he had expended a week of his six-week window—yet another risky move for an important project. The CIO, a former combat officer in Vietnam, was familiar with taking measured risks. His pacing paid off—even with the week to prepare. The team cleared away other projects that could have distracted them and came in ready to work on Monday. They finished the project a day early. Furthermore, they already had their reward, and he didn't have to risk promising them vacation after the project only to have the river (or the CEO) lead him to break his word.

At first glance, as part of an organization rushing hell-bent-for-leather downstream, setting a sane pace seems impossible. It amounts to saying that you should take a leisurely trip over Niagara Falls. Gravity would seem to argue otherwise. But white-water paddlers and experienced managers know ways to control their pace and progress even when the environment races on around you. Being aware of the need to pace yourself constitutes the first step. Building an awareness of when you are going dangerously fast or drowning in change is important. If you recognize the need to control your pace, what should you do about it? The following strategies can help you to pace yourself in a turbulent environment.

> At first glance, as part of an organization rushing hell-bent-for-leather downstream, setting a sane pace seems impossible. It amounts to saying that you should take a leisurely trip over Niagara Falls. Gravity would seem to argue otherwise.

Create a "Not To Do" List

Superhuman exertions or biochemical boosters might help in the short term, but they do not offer a long-term solution to relentless change. You can't keep moving faster as the environment moves faster. You need to recognize your own limits and look at what you can reasonably accomplish—not just what is asked of you. Pacing involves deciding not only what to do, that is, the standard focus of our "to do" lists, but also what *not* to do. You need to decide what part of this roiling mess to engage, and point the nose of your boat in that direction.

The "not to do" list is an easy concept to understand but difficult to implement. It can mean saying "no" to powerful people in the organization or making uncomfortable compromises in standards. You need to demonstrate your effectiveness to make your demand for pacing credible and show that pacing leads to better results. This will give you the ability to say "no" to projects that will push you and your people over the edge. Think of the CFO. Think of the CIO.

You also need to acquire sufficient comfort in laying out explicitly what you can and cannot do—to recognize that as a human being you have limitations, and to work to make others recognize this about both you and them. This doesn't make you a less effective employee. In fact, it means more likely that you will prove a more effective employee over the middle to longer haul. You might disappoint some people in the short run, but you will get more work done, and better work, in the long run. How much does medical leave cost a firm? Or depression? Or divorce? While some may be disappointed today, more people will respect that you know your own limits.

You might object that this pacing isn't possible. Your boss is not going to go away, your kids are not going to go away, and, hopefully, your spouse is not going to go away. You can and should limit debt, maximize savings (especially in retirement accounts), and negotiate severance packages. All of those practices keep you as buoyant as possible. Still, your mortgage payment comes due at the end of the month. There are some things that you cannot say "no" to. But you need to recognize the costs of lost productivity due to exhaustion. You either pay now in confronting those making demands on your time, or you pay later in the impact on your health and performance.

If you believe this is not discussable, that is a problem. You can either hide what you are doing and surreptitiously avoid commitments, or you can make it discussable. Think about how you present it. For example, if you talk to your boss about the pain and suffering of the demands on your time, you might just come off looking like a whiner. But if you come in with information about the costs of exhaustion and overwork or with a plan to alter or reorganize work, you might find a more receptive audience.

If You Think You Can't Do This, You Don't Know Jack

If you think protecting your time in this way will be the end of your career, consider the story a manager at General Electric once told to Greg. Years earlier, as a junior executive, he received a charge to run a cross-functional project for his boss, who was high up in the GE constellation. With this authority, the junior executive began calling leaders from different functions to participate. Most of the calls went well, but then he reached one manager who was not interested. This manager said he didn't have the time.

The junior executive said, "I don't think you understand. My boss said we need to do this, and we need your involvement." The boss was of rank, so it should have carried sufficient weight…or so he thought. But the stubborn manager said that if there were something of importance in it for him, he would move it up on the list. Absent that, he had a lot of important things to do, so he was not going to do this. The junior executive was shocked. That manager, according to the story, was Jack Welch. Drawing the line on what he was willing to do certainly did not stifle his career progress since he became CEO. No one questioned whether Jack Welch worked hard, but he also had the courage and wisdom to draw the line.

> Pacing involves deciding not only
> what to do, that is, the standard
> focus of our "to do" lists, but also
> what *not* to do.

Build Breaks in the Action

New York Yankees Hall of Fame pitcher Lefty Gomez reportedly said, "Never be in a hurry to lose." One of Gomez's greatest rivals was another Hall of Famer, Jimmie Foxx, who played for Yankee archrivals the Philadelphia Athletics and later the Boston Red Sox. Gomez knew that all too often, head-to-head, Foxx outdid the great Gomez. Indeed, Gomez described the powerful Foxx as "having muscles in his hair." One day Gomez found himself facing Foxx late in a close game with several runners on base. The game was at stake, and the screams of tens of thousands of fans emphasized the point. The Yankee catcher went through his signs and Gomez shook them all off. The catcher went through the signs again. Again, Gomez shook them all off. The catcher went through the signs a third time. The stadium throbbed with noise as Gomez shook him off. Three full sets of signs; three full sets rejected.

Puzzled and frustrated, the catcher did something that he did not want to do—he asked the umpire for a time-out and approached the pitching mound. Gomez viewed the mound as his private domain, and his alone. He did not welcome visitors. Before the catcher could reach the mound, Gomez growled, "What are you doing here?" The catcher pointed out that there was a game in progress, that Gomez had only three pitches, and that he had shaken off the catcher's sign three times. He needed to throw the ball. Just what did the great Lefty Gomez want the catcher to do?

Gomez responded gruffly and with diffidence, "Go back behind the plate. I'll pitch when I'm ready. As long as I'm holding the ball, he can't hit it."

Gomez could not make his nemesis vanish. Gomez could not make the situation vanish. He would not walk away. What he could do was to build a break in the action where he could gather his thoughts and concentration. It was all he had left, and he would not relinquish it. The point in business is the same. You may not be able to change the challenges that face you at the plate or change the rules of the game overall, but you can influence how fast you go. No matter how much pressure you face, remember it is your mound. You control your own pace. Never be in a hurry to lose. Slowing down may well affect the outcome and can break the other person's rhythm.

A brief stop for lunch on the river or a pause in an eddy behind a rock can do wonders, renewing your energies for the rapids ahead. For example, on the day that Greg's group of dories was to take on Lava Falls, lunch went long and included time for a siesta—the river would likely prove a bit less turbulent in the afternoon, and the crews definitely more rested for the most challenging of rapids.

During the day and throughout the week, you need to create breaks in the action—perhaps a few moments for reflection or exercise in the morning. It might be a brief meditation before you go to bed to clear the day from your head. You need to enforce and protect these moments, even when the waters are rising. You need places in your life where you can stop and get your bearings, to catch your breath before plunging back into the action. If you think you can live without these breaks, you fool only yourself, and eventually yourself will refuse the fooling. If you think breaks will naturally occur in permanent whitewater or will appear as a reward for all your hard work, you also fool yourself. You need to seek them out. It might mean that you have to take lunch instead of eating at your desk. You might need to respect weekends instead of working straight through them. This is what negotiators call "going to the balcony." Skilled negotiators sense when negotiations stall, and they take a break to step out of the room. This can help break a deadlock or reframe discussions. As in music, sometimes the pauses in the score are the most important part of a performance.

> **You need places in your life where you can stop and get your bearings, to catch your breath before plunging back into the action.**

Get Good Sleep

The previous discussion about sleep deprivation and its impact should make it clear that you need to get more sleep, particularly in a turbulent and stressful environment. But quality of sleep is also important. In *Sleep to Save Your Life*, Dr. Gerard Lombardo offers tips for better sleep, including:[9]

- Get the right amount of sleep for you.
- Keep a regular schedule, based on your responsibilities.
- Relax and give yourself time to unwind. Think evening exercise or a warm bath.
- Create the right environment. Watch how children hold to rituals such as ordering precious stuffed animals or hearing a bedtime story. We suit up to go to work. Find a way to "suit down" to get ready for sleep.
- Use your bedroom for sleeping (and perhaps one other activity). Keep television and bother outside the door.

- Don't go to bed until you are feeling sleepy. Your body says "when." Listen.
- Wake at the same time.
- Do not take naps that interfere with your nighttime sleep (although napping can be useful, as noted in the following section).
- Cut down or eliminate cigarettes, as well as alcohol and caffeine, especially after 4 p.m.
- If you must eat before bedtime, eat sparingly.
- Make peace with the world. Put the hard decisions and conversations off until tomorrow. With those you can, get and give the warmth of a hug, a kiss, or a sincere handshake. Feel the love.

Falling asleep resembles catching a biological or circadian wave. In the end, "at the heart of all sleep problems, whether medical, behavioral, or psychological in origin, is respect for what your body wants to do, which is sleep at certain times of the day and night and be active at others."

Take a Nap

Napping is a bit controversial. Many people associate it with laziness. Some researchers laud naps; others issue some cautions, particularly if it interferes with evening sleep. Surprisingly, some very successful people take "power naps" in the middle of the day. They actually carve out this little peaceful backwater in the middle of a rip-roaring nonstop river. Turn off the BlackBerry, shut the door, and take a 10- to 20-minute nap. We once knew a famous trial lawyer who tucked away an Oriental rug in his office, and most afternoons (when he was not grilling witnesses in court) he unrolled the rug and pulled out a pillow. He closed the door and had his secretary hold all his calls. He found himself more productive afterward just as the research would predict.

Similarly, Greg worked with an executive in his forties in London who had a heart attack as a young man that made him serious about his level of stress and pacing. Every day at his lunch break, he left the office and went to take a short nap. He rose to the top of his function.

Most companies will not actually give you formal napping time or space (although there are a few). So you might have to engage in guerilla napping. If napping in the office proves impossible—particularly if you inhabit a cubicle city—then follow the lead of people keeping a pillow and blanket in the back of the car. Just crawl into this little metal sleep chamber and tilt the seat back. Or you might leave for an appointment or lunch 15 minutes early, taking advantage of a short nap on your arrival. You will arrive at the meeting refreshed (just pack a comb so you don't arrive with bed head). A little creativity will also lead you to find other ways to grab 15 winks when 40 are not possible. A trip for a massage or acupuncture can also offer an opportunity to stretch out and unwind.

If you feel guilty about napping, remember that research shows that people perform better after a nap even if you had a good night's sleep. It also shows that they need less sleep at night. Of course, power napping is no substitute for a solid night's sleep. But when you are flying the red-eye or finishing that late-night project, a nap can provide enough break in the action to help you recharge. You may even live longer. A recent six-year study of Greek adults showed that regular nappers had 37 percent less chance of dying from a heart attack with the benefits appearing especially strong for men.[10]

The rising need to nap has led to a slightly greater social acceptance of napping. Some companies such as Yarde Metals in Southington, Connecticut, allow or encourage "napping on the job." Office furniture retailers are offering napping "furniture" such as napping pods and "fatigue management" products.

If you nap, you will be in good company. Great nappers of history such as Leonardo Da Vinci, Napoleon, Thomas Edison, Albert Einstein, Winston Churchill, and John Kennedy may not have had napping pods or what Deloitte Consulting in Pittsburgh terms "napnasiums," but they knew the benefits of napping. Edison kept a cot in his lab, and Sir Winston said:

> You must sleep some time between lunch and dinner, and no half-way measures. Take off your clothes and get into bed. That's what I always do. Don't think you will be doing less work because you sleep during the day. That's a foolish notion held by people who have no imagination. You will be able to accomplish more. You get two days in one—well, at least one and a half, I'm sure. When the war started, I had to sleep during the day because that was the only way I could cope with my responsibilities.

They also knew how to nap: right length (20 to 30 minutes), right time (not too late so as to affect nighttime sleep patterns), and in a comfortable, quiet spot.

> **If you feel guilty about napping, remember that research shows that people perform better after a nap.**

Enforce Vacations

Kirsten Judd, CEO of the Professional Renewal Center in Lawrence, Kansas, found that most burnt-out patients who came to the center had one thing in common: They never took vacations. Big breaks in the action, truly pulling your boat out of the water, we term vacations. Strangely, many organizations treat vacations as an unwanted cost. While Spain and France mandate that employers give 30 days of vacation per year, and the UK mandates 20, the United States has no mandatory vacation time.[11] The United States lags both in mandatory and in voluntary vacation days. About 50 percent of Americans will not take a real vacation this year.[12] In 2007, an estimated 51 million American employees demured from using all of their vacation days. In effect, they returned almost 438 million days to their employers. Some organizations buy back vacation time as a matter of policy. Evidently, vacations are for wimps, so individuals miss out on the chance to recharge, reorient, and even rethink.

Some organizations lead the way in changing our thinking about vacations. California-based Rand Corporation awards employees who use all their vacation days a 5 percent bonus. Motek, a software firm, offers a set of luggage and $1,000 to any employee taking off three consecutive weeks. PricewaterhouseCoopers created three extra paid holidays by shutting its offices between Christmas Eve and New Year's Day. Furthermore, the firm notifies a supervisor when employees near the forfeit date for use-it-or-lose it vacation days.[13]

In this tough environment, we've imported military imagery to drive people to scale the cliffs and run over the next ridge on the business battlefield. But many organizations have overlooked an important feature of military life—R & R. (And part of the agony of Iraq is the conscious violation of this principle as well.) The military traditionally has been very conscious of pacing and burnout. They push people to the limits (and beyond), but then give them time off. After a stint on the front, a soldier gets a furlough or a desk job. But in business, you are more than likely sent to another front, demanding more peak performance.

Professional athletes peak for seasons and take respites from their grueling regimens. Professional managers need to do so as well.

You need to give yourself sufficient time to get completely away from your work and immersed in something else, so you can come back to the task refreshed. Do you have any hobbies? If not, this might be a sign that you are completely immersed in your work. This is not necessarily a bad thing, but it is a small step from immersion to drowning, so beware. As the example of our CIO shows, it may appear crazy to take a vacation when you have so much work to do, but, in reality, it could be even crazier not to.

In this connected age, you also have to decide where to draw the line on technology when you are on vacation. If you keep reading e-mail, you might not actually have a vacation—you'll just have taken your office with you. You might decide to do some limited work. For example, some managers will read e-mails but not open attachments, which helps limit the amount of work you do but avoids returning to thousands of unread messages or missing responding to a real crisis.

Some of the relentless pace of e-mail is because people don't use their assistants or filtering effectively. Some managers have their assistants handle phone calls, faxes, letters, and every other form of communication but keep the e-mail completely open. Assistants should screen and filter e-mail to keep only the important things coming to you.

> In this tough environment, we've imported military imagery to drive people to scale the cliffs and run over the next ridge on the business battlefield. But many organizations have overlooked an important feature of military life—R & R.

Avoid the Perils of the Crazy Brave and Phony Tough

A crazy environment often brings out the craziness in people. During the Watergate scandal, *Newsweek* columnist Stewart Alsop once characterized the recklessness and swaggering, John Wayne-style bravado of those involved as "crazy brave and phony tough." These two stances can make turbulent environments more dangerous for one and all.

The "crazy brave" are thrill seekers in rivers and organizations who enter turbulent environments and can do some extraordinary things at times. But they ultimately crash and burn—and do a lot of damage to people and organizations around them. Throughout his career, General George Armstrong Custer took extraordinary risks personally and with his command. His fearlessness helped him rise to become the second youngest general in the history of the U.S. Army. At Gettysburg and again near Appomattox, for example, he successfully hurled his greatly outnumbered forces at Lee's army. But a decade later, his fearlessness became recklessness at the Little Big Horn. He raced ahead of other troops in the expedition and ignored reports and caution from his own scouts. He could have waited for a far greater force to arrive, as planned. Instead, he led his men forward into his disastrous "last stand." Crazy brave, they went flying over the falls.

Soccer star Zinedine Zidane was kept out of the first two matches of the World Club playoffs in 2002 by a thigh injury. He probably should have stayed out. Instead, he made the crazy brave move of coming back in the third game. He was not the same player. France lost in the first round without even scoring a goal. He didn't do them any favor by coming back. Bravely overcoming challenges is one thing. Endangering yourself and others by being crazy brave or phony tough is another.

Similarly, in business, you have the "crazy brave" Enron executives who took their entire organization over the waterfalls as they pushed the limits of running the business. Many organizations have high-performing managers whose personal recklessness threatens their own careers and perhaps the organization as a whole. A turbulent environment provides encouragement for this craziness for the "big play," so you need to watch out for this tendency in yourself and in others.

In addition to the crazy brave, a perhaps less obvious and more insidious problem is the "phony tough." These are the people who brag that they work 18 hours a day and have done it for five years without taking breaks. They push themselves to exhaustion, far beyond the point of optimal or even decent performance. The phony tough will start to make mistakes, mistakes that can seriously affect the future of the entire organization. And these phony tough, with their increasingly empty big talk, stand just one double dare away from being crazy brave.

Skilled explorers and paddlers know that their work is to manage the inevitable risks, not seek them out unnecessarily. While a whitewater environment provides inevitable excitement, it requires careful planning, sharp reflexes, and true courage, rather than a swaggering machismo or desire for thrills. As Clint Eastwood's Mr. Dunn in *Million Dollar Baby* would say, "Tough is not enough."

Losing It in the Thirteenth Round

Boxer Billy Conn was tough enough. On June 18, 1941, he entered the ring to face Joe Louis, reigning heavyweight champion of the world. Conn knew it would be a tough fight. Louis outweighed Conn by at least 35 pounds and was legendary in his ability to hit hard and to finish off his opponents. Conn had chosen to fight "up" in weight partly because Louis had run out of heavyweights to fight (having beaten them all) and partly because Conn had a chance, however slim, to outbox Joe Louis. Conn had proven himself a tough and skillful boxer. If Conn could avoid Louis's power, then possibly, just possibly, Conn could pull the upset of upsets and win the bout, the title, and a place in boxing history by outpointing Louis.

Through 12 rounds, Billy Conn did just that; he outboxed the great Joe Louis. He even buckled the champ's knees several times and probably came within a hair of knocking Louis down in the twelfth round. Then, in round 13, Billy Conn stopped boxing and started slugging. He went toe to toe with Joe Louis. Conn's corner vociferously entreated him to return to boxing, to the careful accumulation of points, but Conn wanted more than a victory; he wanted a knock-out. He got one. Joe Louis knocked Billy Conn into a near fetal position on the canvas. In a post-fight interview, a reporter asked Conn why he had changed tactics in the thirteenth round, to which Conn replied, "What's the sense of being Irish if you can't be thick?"

Decades later, Conn and Louis participated in a panel of heavy-weight fighters. Conn jabbed at Louis saying, "I could have been champ." Louis counterpunched, "You were...for 12 rounds." Billy Conn was more than tough enough to win. Billy Conn was more than smart enough (witness his smart investment of his boxing earnings and comfortable lifestyle). Billy Conn went outside him-self—outside what he was best at—just when he needed to stay within himself. By "being thick," he went crazy brave.

If not craziness or toughness, then what does it take to succeed in this environment? The factors that will lead to success are, on the surface, far more mundane: the right skills, the right equipment, and the right mindset. The ocean-liner organizations that took us across great patches of open water have already broken apart, and we have launched the lifeboats of more nimble organizational units without the grand ballrooms and corner offices.

The environment has certainly grown crazier, but this doesn't mean you need to become phony tough or crazy brave. You need to find a way to navigate through the turbulence. You need the flexibility and responsiveness designed for true whitewater. This environment can be exhausting and unforgiving. You need to control your pace and balance courage with humility.

> The "crazy brave" are thrill seekers in rivers and organizations who enter turbulent environments and can do some extraordinary things at times. But they ultimately crash and burn.

KEEP A ROLL IN RESERVE

Your mother told you to take care of yourself, to eat right, and to get thee to a doctor when symptoms dictate. She was right...of course. A tired or ill kayaker is a danger to him- or herself as well as to others. Few of us can play at 20 percent below peak and keep up, let alone 30 to 50 percent below peak. How many times have you seen a star athlete limp onto a field only to be outdone by an average athlete? Yes, many of us can recall a star such as Mickey Mantle or Kirk Gibson limping to the plate, hitting a game-winning homer, and then limping around the bases, or Curt Schilling, blood oozing from his surgically cobbled together ankle, pitching brilliantly to help the Red Sox overcome "The Curse." It can happen...with the right circumstances—for example, you only have to bat, so limited mobility does not matter, or a long and restorative post-season awaits, or world-class doctors have done the cobbling and literally stand by to intervene.

Imagine that you and I compete for clients around the country or around the world. You are better than I am. You are smarter and better trained. You also believe that you are the second coming of Superman. You book long trips back to back. You fly from LA to New York on the red-eye for a sales call and then to Miami for the next day.

Me? I acknowledge more of my limits. I rarely schedule key client meetings on back-to-back days in cities three or more time zones apart. I plan to do my prep on the ground so that travel time amounts to "found time." I seldom go a week without at least four cardiovascular workouts. I make sure that I'm never away from home more than eight nights a month and never more than three in any week. I sleep with my spouse more nights than not and have no fewer than seven meals a week with my family. My dog and my toddler recognize me immediately.

I am usually at the top of my game while you are usually performing 10 to 30 percent below your peak. Yes, you are smarter and better trained than I am. You are just dumber in how you leverage what you've got. We meet ten times in the marketplace, and I win at least six and probably seven or eight times. I am not better than you. I do not have to be. I just have to be better at game time.

Turbulence can kill suddenly, but perhaps its greatest danger comes from its ability to wear you down over time. Day after day of fighting rapids can deplete energy and exhaust attention. Paddlers late in the day are more likely to make foolish mistakes and to lack the strength to recover from them. Paddler Jeff Bennett described kayaking the Upper Kings River in California at a very high level as "a long stretch of Class V rapids *leading into the bad stuff.*" Just 3 miles into their trip, they found that "our fun meters were pegged, and our energy levels were low." When they pulled out to scout the next run, within 30 minutes, "half the crew had their sleeping bags spread out and dinner on the stove."

Experienced paddlers try not to play themselves out. They always make sure they keep some energy in reserve for the unexpected—energy for that last roll you might need to make in a pinch. They realize that complete exhaustion greatly reduces your options. They control their momentum down the river so they can see what is coming. They recognize that using these reserves might mean flirting with death. Because you don't know what challenges you will face, you conserve some margin of error—and if you have consumed it, then get off the river.

In your work, you also need to build in a similar margin of safety. You need to have a sane enough pace so that you can deal with the inevitable turbulence you will encounter. Instead of just looking at your current work, ask yourself: What happens if my company announces a merger next week? What if my business unit is reorganized? What if I need to move to a new office? What if my job responsibilities are increased? What if my current job goes to India and I need to find a new one? What if a competitor's move requires a rapid response? This permanent whitewater environment could kick up any of these events. Consequently, think marathon, not sprint. Do you have the capacity to deal with these shocks if they happen to you? To the extent that you can, pace yourself to keep a bit of energy in reserve for such predictable "surprises." Find the eddies where you can get your bearings and recover. When you face pressure, as Billy Joel says, "you have to learn to pace yourself."

> Experienced paddlers try not to play themselves out. They always make sure they keep some energy in reserve for the unexpected.

THE TAKEOUT

Relentless, permanent whitewater often doesn't provide any natural breaks in the action. You cannot trust the environment to provide a manageable pace,[1] so you need to pace yourself.

CHAPTER 3

Mastering the Roll
Prepare to Fail Gracefully and Recover Quickly

Far better it is to dare mighty things, to win glorious triumphs,
even though checkered by failure, than to take rank with those
poor spirits who neither enjoy much nor suffer much, because
they live in the gray twilight that knows not victory or defeat.
—*Theodore Roosevelt*

A consultant received a phone call from a CEO who said that he wanted to transform the culture of his organization. They spoke for a bit, and the consultant expressed an interest in continuing the conversation. He offered to pay for his travel and to buy dinner (but not alcohol) for the CEO and his management team at the most expensive restaurant near their headquarters, with one small caveat that he would share at dinner.

The senior staff immediately leaned into the task at hand with great vigor. After all, few executives would pass on the opportunity to fleece a consultant! Reconnaissance teams, deployed throughout the culinary vicinity, foraged for menus and especially for prices. Additionally, several senior executives took this as the opportunity to add that designer suit or dress to their wardrobe—what better time to drop four figures on an Armani something!

People arrived at the chosen elegant restaurant finely turned out and in the best of moods. They walked past staff with the haughty air too frequently associated with such establishments. The executives paid them little mind, however, and took their seats. This would be fun. The triple linen tablecloths and genuine silver place settings indicated just how much this evening would cost the consultant. The food, the company, the treat would combine to create a most enjoyable experience and memorable story.

After a little small talk, the consultant restated his commitment to pay for his travel and for dinner sans alcohol. Smiles of contented satisfaction spread across the faces of senior staff. Then, he laid out his caveat: *no forks*.

Some grumbling ensued, but the silver forks (many of them!) were reluctantly stacked at the center of the linen tablecloth, never to be touched again. The salads came out, and the executives awkwardly picked up their spoons and knives. Lettuce slid over the sides of their bowls. Arugula fell to the tablecloth between bowl and mouth. Croutons bounced into their laps. The executives cast sideways glances at their hapless colleagues, who were faring no better. They stared with unexpected desire at the stack of forks in the middle of the table before concentrating again on the disaster in front of them. Finally, the ragged remains of the salads were mercifully carted off, like stretchers from a battlefield. The bemused and at least moderately annoyed waiters did their best to dab up the dressing that had been carpet-bombed across the white tablecloth. It was not a pretty sight, and the night was young.

There was a brief pause in the foxholes, but then came wave after wave of intricately prepared food. The executives manhandled each course in turn. The main course arrived, and the scene repeated. They began cutting their steak and chicken, pinning the meat with the edge of a spoon while sawing with the knife. Chateaubriand slid around their plates, and bits of meat flew off the sides. String beans were balanced precariously across spoons like logs on a forklift. There were more glances of longing toward the silver forks. An ordinarily easy and enjoyable meal had become difficult work. The executives had never known until that moment how much they depended on forks, and their best, expensive, and in some cases recently and specially chosen clothes were the worse for the various slips twixt cup and lip.

The senior executives also felt the keen edge of social exposure and disapproval. The waiters had moved from haughty bemusement to scorn at the table manners and mess. The diners imagined, and not without cause, that the waiters were discussing them—that is, the barbarians at the center table. Additionally, one member of the party became aware of a professional associate and friend dining at a nearby table. The forkless diner suddenly became preoccupied with the question of repairing social reputation.

At the end of the meal, the consultant looked around this circle of grim faces and calmly asked how they felt. "Incompetent," said one executive. "Vulnerable," said another. "Embarrassed." "Angry." The group quickly redirected its anger from the meal toward the consultant. What was the point of this exercise? Was it just to make us look foolish? Is this any way to treat a potential client?

The consultant took his bashing calmly. Then he explained that the set of sweeping changes these leaders proposed in their organization amounted to asking employees to give up their forks. Namely, employees would have to give up behaviors and skills developed over a lifetime, behaviors and skills that allowed people to perform their jobs competently. These change leaders would, in effect, be asking employees to place their forks, those hard won behaviors and skills, in the middle of their respective desks and then get on with performing their jobs.

Their reports would feel what the company's leaders felt at that table. They too would feel discomfort, incompetence, vulnerability, and downright foolishness. The would-be change agents were asking their employees to live without their "forks," the forks they had become accustomed to and used every day. The entire organization would experience the same emotions as the executives had that night. Furthermore, as the senior executives had directed their frustration and anger at the consultant, the "cause" of the emotions, so would organizational members direct their frustration and anger at senior executives, the "cause" of their emotions.

"Do you understand what you are getting into here?" the consultant asked. "This is personal. This is change."

> At the end of the meal, the consultant looked around this circle of grim faces and calmly asked how they felt. "Incompetent," said one executive. "Vulnerable," said another. "Embarrassed." "Angry."

FAILURE IS THE ONLY OPTION

The evening highlighted an important truth: Change means trying new things and failing. It means vulnerability and frustration to the point of anger. It means suffering. It means getting comfortable hanging upside down in your boat, under the icy water, without oxygen. It means hanging in there and continuing to function even when you look and feel foolish. And then rolling back up. It means failing and then recovering to continue on, and then failing again.

Business is about avoiding mistakes. We all want to appear competent. We want our forks. Success means knowing what to do and getting the job done. So we struggle with the idea that *failing* is part of the job of change. It is okay for kids, but once you stop being a toddler, it is no longer "cute" to fall over while walking down the hallway. It is no longer funny to see the disaster around your plate after eating without forks.

The crew of a traditional boat or ship would define failure as capsizing. No one wants to be captain of the *Titanic*, as failure is seen from the deck of a capsizing ocean liner. On the ocean liner, the ship goes down only once. Your first capsize is your last, and it is a disaster. The organization waits for someone to collect the survivors in lifeboats. Recovery falls to treasure hunters in biospheres decades later. And the captain usually looks for a different line of work, on land.

The world looks different from the deck of a kayak. In turbulent environments, capsizing is not only an option—it is an inevitability. You don't win by fighting capsizing because you see it as failure. Rather, you plan to capsize. You practice how to minimize it. You learn to Eskimo roll so that when the water flips you over you know how to recover gracefully. Failure is part of the process. Whitewater kayaks are not particularly stable. This means that they can be flipped more easily, but it also means that they can be rolled back up more easily.

Without an Eskimo roll, however, a trip down a whitewater river can seem similar to capsizing on an ocean liner. If you flip and fail to make your roll in a kayak, you have to pop your spray skirt and swim for shore. It is always wet, often cold. Sometimes fellow paddlers will help, but you typically face a bewildering swim through rushing water—sucked under and popped back up, knocked against rocks—before you find land. Then you have to drag your tail out of the river and empty the water out of your boat, climb back in, put on your spray skirt, and continue on your way—until you hit the next wave right around the corner. Such "bagels" (a roll with a hole in it) typically amount to only an inconvenience. However, in some places on some rivers such a swim could prove fatal. In any event, it is an exhausting and humiliating process, as fellow paddlers watch from the current. If you do this once or twice, you have a very strong incentive to perfect your roll.

While you expect to fail, you don't take foolish risks. You need to know your skills and your limits. You try your best to avoid failures that could be fatal by knowing which are which. But if you don't flip on the river, you are just not trying hard enough or experimenting with tough challenges. Also, you are probably not having nearly enough fun. The only true failure in whitewater is not to be prepared to recover from failure.

Even if you are a stellar employee, your career will hit periods when you capsize through no fault of your own. You may find yourself in a bewildering new job, with a new boss, in a new organization, or out on the street. You can't avoid this. It is just the way it is in whitewater. Since you can't avoid it, you need to cultivate the ability for quick and efficient recovery from the inevitable disasters. You need to view iteration as a way of life, moving away from seeing your accomplishments as rungs on a career ladder to seeing them as journeys through different rapids or different rivers.

When you shoot rapids, at some point you will find yourself underwater. That fact probably qualifies as the only certainty in a turbulent environment. Clinging to the belief that you can avoid these spills is often more dangerous than accepting them. Recovery skills for turbulent environments are similar to the Eskimo roll in kayaking (see sidebar, "Failing Gracefully: The Eskimo Roll"). Once you have these recovery skills, you can paddle into big water without fear of being capsized or tossed about. You know you can always regain your center and come back up. You will expect to make mistakes and get your hair wet. You will feel no horror, or shame, or embarrassment (except for the dreaded "helmet head" when your wet hair snakes out of the holes in your helmet). Sure you are upside down. This is what is supposed to happen in whitewater. It is all in a day's work. And you know how to recover to bring yourself back into the air. You've been eating without forks for so long that you don't flinch even when they take away your spoons.

> ## The only failure in whitewater is not to be prepared to recover from failure.

FAILING GRACEFULLY: THE ESKIMO ROLL

In kayaking, the Eskimo roll (a maneuver to bring the boat upright after it has capsized) is one of the most important ways to prepare for the inevitable "failure" of flipping over. Why is it important to learn to roll? A successful roll keeps you in the boat, rather than outside where you face a difficult or dangerous rescue in the middle of a rushing river. It allows you to recover quickly from mistakes so you can take more risks and have more fun playing. This provides the difference between a small interruption or a long swim. In some cases, it can mean the difference between life and death. If you play and experiment, then you will flip many times in the course of a day. But it is no big deal. You just roll back up. Through a simple combination of paddle movements and hip actions, you can right your boat with very little effort. In fact, it requires so little effort that experienced kayakers can come up without using a paddle at all—a hands roll.

In organizations in turbulent environments, failure is inevitable. You will find yourself in new and unpredictable environments. You need to fail and then recover quickly. Failure is no big deal. Recovery is quick and effortless. Your first instinct in a turbulent organizational environment may be to panic and bail out. You might look for a quiet place in your maze of cubicles to hide. But you have to challenge yourself to live with discomfort, and train yourself to become more comfortable in this uncomfortable environment. Then you can begin to develop effective strategies and responses. The more you practice immersing yourself in change and dealing with it effectively, the more comfortable you can become. You need to learn the strategies—often counterintuitive—that fit this permanent whitewater environment. We all hate to fail, but we can get used to it, minimize its effect, and develop techniques for coming back up.

STRATEGIES FOR FAILING QUICKLY AND RECOVERING GRACEFULLY

How do you cultivate this comfort with uncertainty and failure? How do you build the skills to recover gracefully? To meet this environment, you need to change your strategies and mindset. You can't prevent failure. You can treat your career as a series of experiments. You can minimize the risk of disastrous consequences from failure and increase your learning from it.

Treat Your Career as a Series of Experiments

Instead of moving from success to success, you can view your career as a series of experiments—some of which will fail. When an experiment in a lab does not produce the expected result, the researcher is not usually heartbroken. The failure merely shows one more thing that doesn't work. Look at your career the same way and you will focus less on perfection today than on building skills for tomorrow. The environment will not permit you to succeed all the time. You can be the best at what you do, but a merger or acquisition can rock your world by completely reshaping your organization. You can be a dynamite programmer in today's language, but the language may change or the work may move to India. Failure merely signals that it is time to launch some new experiments.

The young employee who sees a career as a steady climb will shudder when rungs are missing or the ladder disappears. The experimenter will realize this one route upward didn't work and promptly switch to exploring other routes. This will lead to a more open mind about the possibilities rather than a single-minded devotion to a path that doesn't work. More experienced managers who must always be right and successful will not explore new ways to apply their skills or build new ones. As the world changes, this can lead to Willie Loman syndrome, as suffered by Arthur Miller's character in *Death of a Salesman*, who is left behind by a changing world. As Miller said in a 2001 interview in *Humanities* magazine, "a lot of people give a lot of their lives to a company or even the government, and when they are no longer needed, when they are used up, they're tossed aside... . Willie Loman's situation is even more common now than it was then. . . . I've gotten a number of letters from people who were in pretty good positions at one point or another and then were just peremptorily discarded."[1]

A need exists in this permanent whitewater world for continuous learning and even rethinking work or careers. If you were starting anew, what are the possibilities for someone with your set of skills? Where could you launch your boat on new rivers? How could you conduct experiments to test the waters in these areas? Where are the opportunities to take small risks, small experiments, that can change the way you look at your life and work?

> When an experiment in a lab does not produce the expected result, the researcher is not usually heartbroken. The failure merely shows one more thing that doesn't work. Look at your career the same way and you will focus less on perfection today than on building skills for tomorrow.

Minimize the Risk of Failure

First, work your way up to the big water. Start with runs on a Class I river with easy rapids. Develop your skill and your comfort. Then, move to Class II, then III, then IV, or more. One can master the basic skills of navigating the water and understanding its dynamics in a place where failure only means a swim, not a deadly descent into a rapid called Meat Grinder or a visit to the underside of an undercut rock. When you gain the skills from the small, but inevitable, failures (and successes!), you can take on more serious water. Developing yourself takes time and discipline.

Second, be honest about the true risks. A paddler Rob knew once brought his girlfriend along rafting on the Class IV New River in West Virginia. She had never paddled whitewater before, let alone something like this. He told her the waves she'd encounter were "just like the ocean." She quickly realized that the chaos she was battling through was *nothing* like the ocean. She was drenched, terrified, shivering, and more than a little bit miffed by the time she reached the takeout. People need to know what they are getting into and to be sure they have the skills to meet it. Also, be honest about your own capabilities...and those of others. If you haven't done something like this before, ask for advice from others so you have a shot at being successful—or at least surviving. Informed choice requires mindfulness, honesty, and collaboration.

Third, find a way to fail that doesn't kill you. Betting the ranch does not make for successful failure. Entrepreneurs know this truth. For example, successful entrepreneurs avoid betting the whole load. If they fail, they prefer to "fail fast and fail cheap." Successful entrepreneurs take calculated risks. Instead of leaving the private sector for a nonprofit, try becoming a board member of a small or nonprofit organization. You can get close enough to see if it is a good fit without putting your whole career at risk. If you want to move in a new direction, figure out what percentage of your time you should invest in this, and treat it like a risky financial investment. Even daredevils do not necessarily take crazy risks. Evil Knievel discussed how carefully he planned his jumps. He calculated risks even when attempting to jump rows of buses or the Grand Canyon.

Fourth, make sure that you pack your own chute. Remember the basics:

- Negotiate a sound employment contract on the way in, when you are on a roll, and when the labor market is hot.
- Keep your personnel file updated. Know what is in it and add concrete laudatory notes whenever possible. If your company won't keep the file, then find someone who will.
- Live prudently. Make sure that you have access to money to keep you afloat for at least six months (ideally, savings).
- Get out and about. Conferences, trade shows, and executive education provide the opportunity to learn as well as to see and be seen.

- Visit Monster.com and similar sites to stay abreast of opportunities. Consider checking employment agencies and headhunters *before* you need them.
- Think cell phone, call centers, and Internet and what you can do with those dominant and evolving technologies.

> Find a way to fail that doesn't kill you. Betting the ranch does not make for successful failure. Entrepreneurs know this truth.

Master the Emotions of Failure

Failure comes with its own set of difficult emotions. You need to master these emotional forces in your own thinking to maintain a center of balance. Confront and master your fears. In golf, if you are afraid of putting the ball in the woods or trees, some golf pros recommend teeing up as close as possible to the side of the obstacle. It allows you to move beyond your fear to the challenge at hand. Leaders, for example, benefit from experiencing failure or near failure early in their careers. A crucible helps them to learn concrete skills. More important, the experience teaches them about leading themselves through trying times. Next time the water churns heavily, they can employ their hard-won skills to the challenge at hand, without the turbulence of their own psychodynamics.

> Leaders benefit from experiencing
> failure or near failure early
> in their careers.

Practice Failing

Unfortunately, you cannot avoid failing or minimize it away, so you also need to improve how you fail. Kayakers spend their winters in swimming pools, practicing rolling their boats, working on offside rolls, and honing their reflexes. Basic technique matters. High-potential employees benefit greatly from receiving true challenges, challenges that will stretch them and give them the possibility of failure. One needs the experience of at least near-failure to practice handling one's self amidst the emotional crosscurrents associated with the specter of failure. These career disasters, planned or unplanned, teach important lessons. People need to know what it feels like when your knuckles turn white. They feel the hot breath of the wolf of failure on their necks. If they don't have that experience, they don't learn, and they aren't prepared for leadership—of others or of themselves.

The goal is to come up with a challenge that brings the wolf right up to the back of the person's neck, without drawing blood. Venture capitalists know to look for entrepreneurs made wiser by failure, and often won't invest with people who have not experienced failure. These leaders have survived the crucible. They know more about making a business work than entrepreneurs who have moved from success to success. They have lived through what Margaret Thatcher calls those times that put "iron in the spine."

People learn more from a process of "deliberate mistakes" than from successes.[2] In a stable environment, learning may prove important, so getting the job done is the focus. For example, if you ferry across a flat lake every day, then you focus on making the trip as quickly and safely as possible, and with the least fuel. You do the same trip every day, so you get good at that one thing. In contrast, in a turbulent environment, the challenges vary every day. Learning and building your skills so that you can better understand and handle your environment matter more. And, like a pilot working in a flight simulator, you learn more if you make more mistakes. You need flexibility of action and resiliency of character. You may not have faced the particular challenge before, but you have faced similar ones. You have felt the fear and have survived. You have developed flexibility.

High-risk professionals use training as a way to help them to prepare for high-anxiety situations. For soldiers, the drills help to desensitize them to loud noises, human distress, and primitive fears so that they can differentiate amidst the chaos of stimuli and focus on the task at hand. One Vietnam-era Special Forces officer described his "favorite" training exercises. His trainers would fly him around for hours in an airplane with the windows blackened. He had no idea where he was. He didn't even know whether it was day or night. Then they would throw open the door and order him to jump. He jumped. On the way down, he realized it was pitch black. He didn't know whether he was in the United States or Costa Rica. As he went out they handed him the coordinates for his pick-up. Good luck. But when the time came for a real mission, it didn't matter where he went, he was ready. He knew the drill and had the capacity to adjust.

Experienced marriage and relationship counselors know the benefits of failure, for they know that partners who have experienced the pain of a broken heart—failure if you will, of earlier relationships—have a greater likelihood of maintaining successful marriages. Such veterans of intimate relationships know what is at stake and choose to move ahead, better informed about themselves, relationships, and how to tend to a marriage. They know better what they seek and what it will take from them and from others to secure it. They proceed knowing the stakes and the risk. They proceed with hope in the face of their fear.

> Venture capitalists know to look for entrepreneurs made wiser by failure, and often won't invest with people who have not experienced failure. These leaders have survived the crucible. They know more about making a business work than entrepreneurs who have moved from success to success.

Prepare to Learn from Failure

While you need comfort with failure, you also need to try not to make the same mistake twice: Learn from your mistakes. First, adjust your mindset. You have to go from seeing failure as an unthinkable horror to seeing it as an inevitable part of the journey. Take a look at Abraham Lincoln's career. Or study George Washington, especially as a military commander, and his continued dedication to learn and to improve. And Winston Churchill's career underwhelms prior to his rise to lead England through the perilous times of the Second World War.

Second, set out to do something. Learning comes easier if you have a hypothesis to test. Take the journey (and yourself) seriously enough to express and note your hopes and objectives. As the saying goes, fishing starts with throwing in your line. Failure (or success) can only happen in relation to what one sets out to do. So, set out to do.

Third, keep records and debrief. Take the time to re-create the failure and to understand it. While the FAA knows that it cannot prevent all crashes, it installs "black boxes" in aircraft so that it can learn from past mistakes. Install and review your own personal black boxes. Debrief after both successes and failures to find out what went wrong, or right.

Fourth, do not go it alone. Others can provide perspective and support and can help you learn. To get this support, however, you need to find and cherish relations with people capable of helping you when you most need it.

> Learn from your mistakes. Have a
> hypothesis to test. Debrief after
> successes and failures.

Make Your Mistakes on the Move

Amid turbulence, trajectory matters more than exact location. The journey is not linear or predictable. Defining the primary approach to a stretch of a river certainly matters. But, to paraphrase military strategist Carl von Clausewitz, no plan survives contact with the river intact.

Follow the "Pareto principle" of focusing on the key 20 percent of your work or life that will yield 80 percent of the returns. Richard Koch, in *Living the 80/20 Way*, says the key to so much of modern life lies in identifying and pursuing this 20 percent. So much changes so fast that the current washes away the details. Many conscientious, detail-focused people thrived on the ocean liner and yet struggle to recognize that leading themselves and others turns on the 20 percent that yields 80 percent.

Edward M. Hallowell delivers a complementary message in *CrazyBusy*.[3] Hallowell delineates many of the traps waiting to distract and exhaust us. Many of the traps we have created ourselves through adopting connecting technologies such as e-mail, cellular phones, and BlackBerries. Others we have created by allowing the technological froth to interfere with our vital and nourishing connection to others and to ourselves. We have moved farther from Walden Pond, but Thoreau's counsel to "simplify, simplify, simplify" has never seemed more apt or more difficult.

Locate what matters and move toward it. Failure to locate what matters increases the likelihood of getting lost. The froth comes to dominate. Being lost in whitewater carries fundamental risks—literally not knowing up (stream) from down (stream) in a rapid can lead to exhaustion, injury, and even death. More mundanely, being lost hampers learning and undercuts resilience. Making progress or not depends on where one is headed. Learning, calibrating, re-energizing, and developing require relative movement toward that desired point.

Take a long view. We've all probably met teenagers who think their lives ended once they failed (or succeeded) in getting into their first-choice college. They think it amounts to a sort of finish line that determines winners and losers or happiness and sadness from then on. They don't realize that they have barely started. The river keeps rolling, holding the possibility of a thousand more flips and rolls, a thousand more opportunities if you just keep paddling.

For too many, especially for too many of the talented, exhaustion takes over and the desire to journey dies. The head of a major clinical program at a national academic center volunteered to Greg recently that the biggest problem that he had in awarding various prestigious fellowships centered on finding people in their twenties with any spark left. Or, as he said, "they have great, even incredible resumes, but they're done. The lights have gone out."

No sprint this, but a marathon. Training, pace, and perspective all matter. A longer view helps you learn. A setback is just a setback taken against the backdrop of a lifetime. As Seth Godin points out in his book *The Dip*, successes and failures alike start with a period of difficulties. It often is hard to tell which one is which—until you travel further downstream. You need to recognize when to power through these dips to get to the upside of the curve, when to ride with them, and when to bail out. Keep a trajectory and, above all, keep moving.

> Take a long view. The river keeps rolling, holding the possibility of a thousand more flips and rolls, a thousand more opportunities if you just keep paddling.

FAILING AND PLAY

Failing and playing are cousins. Failing involves a serious attempt to succeed in the face of risk. The main difference between failing and playing is the level of the consequences. Unless you are playing at the Roman coliseum, games usually involve loss of face but not loss of life. On the blackjack table you may bet a few dollars, but in business you may bet your career or personal wealth. Both failure and play involve trial and potential embarrassment. Play focuses more on the process than the end product.

Being able to fail gracefully and to recover quickly reduces the risks of play. A paddler who can roll is less at risk than one who has to swim. This means the paddler who can roll can afford a less conservative approach *and* have more fun. If you don't have a roll, every time you try to play you will be flipped and swim. Skills in recovering from failure are essential in finding ways to play and meeting turbulence with optimism, which is the focus of Chapter 4, "The Power of Play: Optimism and Resilience."

 THE TAKEOUT

Failure is not tragedy. Failure is a fact of life in turbulent environments. Get used to it, minimize the risks, and develop strategies to recover quickly.

CHAPTER 4

The Power of Play
Optimism and Resilience

There comes a time on the water when you feel as though you know where every bubble is, sense every current, instinctively time each surge, and smoothly absorb its power. And at last you will be set free, gliding gently and serenely in the midst of apparent chaos, with the sunlight sparkling in the spray all around. This is the alchemy of play-paddling—becoming enveloped in the music and magic of flowing water.[1]
—Doug Ammons, "certified play paddler"

We work in a wild, but also potentially invigorating, world. Greg once asked a group of managers from a major telecommunications firm—in the midst of the vortex of deregulation—if their jobs were harder than before. Almost every hand went up. No surprise there. They had experienced waves of acquisitions, reorganizations, and regulatory changes, year after year.

The surprise came with the response to his next question: "Do you like your job more?" Almost all their hands went up again. They found their work more difficult, *and* more enjoyable. They were excited because they had more discretion. They had more variety. They didn't know what they would face on any given day. These managers would say: "The job is a lot more fun. I just wish there were not *so much* of it."

> When managers from a major telecommunications firm were asked about their work, they said: "The job is a lot more fun. I just wish there were not so much of it."

THE PLAY'S THE THING

Whitewater paddlers would understand this sentiment. With the right skills and equipment, they play in waters that others avoid. Whitewater paddlers are like otters. Playing is the whole point of the exercise. They plunge into roiling holes, surf along crashing waves, and do all kinds of tricks, most of which involve being shot in the air, splashed in the face, or flipped under water. There are "enders" or "pop-ups" where the kayaker points the nose of a boat into a wave or hole. The downstream water pushes on the front deck of the boat while upstream water pushes on the bottom and the whole boat goes vertical. At times, the paddler can balance on the nose of the boat, twirling around in a "pirouette," like a dancer or a trained dolphin at Sea World.

Paddlers side surf holes, leaning sideways into a hole (improbably held across the current in an upstream blackflow like the currents below a small waterfall), and then spin the boat in circles to do "donuts" or "spins." Playboaters do "bow stalls" standing on their noses (and even bounce up and down balanced there), "stern squirts," shooting up in the air from the back deck, "cartwheels," and many much wilder rodeo moves. There are obscure combination moves with names that would make a video gamer or snowboarder salivate—such as "Phoenix monkey" or "McNasty."

Paddling downstream, kayakers "boof" over submerged rocks, and, for a little added excitement, they will sometimes run waterfalls.

If this isn't entertaining enough, kayakers do all these moves with small hand paddles or just hands alone. Rob even once came across a group of boaters on the New River in West Virginia who were reportedly running with hand paddles without any clothes beneath their spray skirts—so if they had to swim, there would be added fun!

It is important to remember that kayakers do all this on rivers that most people would consider about as far from "fun" as one could imagine. In fact, most people seeing these rivers for the first time might consider them *dangerous*. They might have flashbacks of *Deliverance*. If someone tossed you into these rapids, fun might be the last thing on your mind, as survival moved front and center.

> With the right skills and equipment, they play in waters that others avoid. Playing is the whole point of the exercise.

 ## PLAYING A HOLE: FINDING A STILL POINT IN THE MIDST OF CHAOS

When water flows rapidly over a submerged rock or other obstruction, it flows back upstream to create a "hole" or hydraulic where the upstream backflow and downstream current meet. This is similar to the backflow below a water-fall, on a slightly smaller scale. Placing the boat in this hole, a paddler can sit stationary across the flow of the river and surf while the water races around the boat. The water goes very rapidly downstream on all sides, but the boat remains stationary. In organizations, you can find such sweet spots within the turbulence. Perhaps you cannot reduce the turbulence or find a quiet backwater for rest, but you can keep from being swept downstream.

In the organization, engaging and attractive projects might equate to such play holes. With your heart and will engaged in the process, you more willingly spend the time and energy to make the project a success. This is where the hard work becomes play. The key is to avoid projects that are "keepers," the kind that suck you in like the backwash of a waterfall and won't spit you out, or the "losers" that just sweep you along.

You need to choose holes (or projects at work) that captivate you, but still allow you to make an exit when you are exhausted. Finding the right ones requires understanding your own skills and stamina as well as the depth and power of the hole (or project) itself. When you find one that challenges but does not overwhelm you, it can be one of the best spots to be in a turbulent environment. Chaos is all around you, and yet you are surfing at the still point in the storm.

In today's turbulent work environment, you might think that you can only hunker down and try to get through these brutal rapids. Keep your head down and the turmoil will stop soon. Yet, it won't. If you look closely, if you develop the right mindset—particularly optimism—build skills such as resilience, and find the right equipment, you can actually have more fun in this environment than any other. The younger generation recognizes this. Author Donald Tapscott, who has conducted extensive research on the Net Generation, identified "play" as one of the norms of this new wired generation. They expect work to be engaging and interactive—in other words, less like what their older peers might call "work" and more like "play." Maybe we can learn something from them.

The more turbulence you have in your environment, the more trouble you have—and the more likely that these troubled waters will contain great play spots. The river churns water in new patterns and takes organizations in new directions. This creates a rich environment. You will fail more in such a world, but you will also have many more opportunities to play. The numerous testimonials to positive life changes stemming from many layoffs and the accompanying choices bear evidence that such a possibility exists.

You need to know when to play and when not to play. Hint: Not when you drop the cooling rods into the reactor. But play spawns creativity. It is a vital component of our lives and of our organizations. Being at play means being childlike in openness, wonder, and delight. Such is the stuff of creativity, but it is also the stuff of renewal and resilience. As Salvador Dali once said, "You have to systematically create confusion. It releases creativity." In whitewater, the turbulence can be a descent into hell or an opportunity for play. This is the Rorschach test of modern work life. What do you see when you look into the waves?

> **If you develop the right mindset—particularly optimism—build skills such as resilience, and find the right equipment, you can actually have more fun in this environment than any other.**

THE POWER OF OPTIMISM

Ernest Shackleton's ship was gone. He was stranded with his crew on the floating, melting ice in the desolate Antarctic. His plan to cross Antarctica was dashed. Now, they would be lucky to survive. He had optimism, but not much else.

For several months, the ice had gripped his ship and slowly crushed it. He had made his share of mistakes. He had chosen to press on despite warnings of massive ice floes. He had chosen to stop the engines for fear of consuming too much coal (and failed to stock more coal in the first place). Neither had he stocked dynamite that might have blasted open a passage. His ship was literally sinking at the edge of Antarctica. They were 346 miles from the nearest food dump. No outsider knew or could know their situation. After all, it was October 25, 1915, and they were about 11 months and a world removed from any human habitation with no hope of radio contact. Shackleton matter-of-factly gave the order to abandon ship. They set up camp on the ice. He gathered his expedition about him and said, as he wrote in his journal, simply, "ship and stores have gone—so now we'll go home."

Numerous miscalculations and failures did not defeat Shackleton. He demonstrated at least three behavioral tendencies of successful leaders at such a juncture: optimism or the demonstrated belief that you can do something, that there is reason to hope; action orientation, that doing supersedes not doing or trying; and tenacity—evidence of sticking with it, of not folding just because of hard times. Another move remains. Make it. As we all know, Shackleton's tenacious optimism contributed mightily to one of the most extraordinary self-rescues in the history of polar exploration, indeed, in the history of the world. All of his men, improbably, made it safely back to civilization.

Working to maintain optimism amounts in many ways to swimming upstream against powerful societal currents. We have become a society of victims. The rise of industrial society, with the growth of social science and psychology, shifted attribution of behavior from the individual to the environment. Often, we see people as a product of environment or of a genetic roll of the dice. This trivialization of individuals and their respective efforts to adapt can lead easily to fatalism, a sense that "the fix is in" (at birth or by age seven or so). This can breed depression and passivity. This "modern" view of humans as victims may fit a world of episodic change (a steady state/change/steady state world), but it hamstrings anyone living in permanent whitewater. The point here is not that genetics and environment do not matter. They do. However, the way you approach the world greatly influences the way that you experience and act on the world. You can change your approach. As Jack Nicholson's character in *The Departed* says, in a rather perverse embodiment of this approach, "I don't want to be a product of my environment. I want my environment to be a product of me."

> **Numerous miscalculations and failures did not defeat Shackleton. He showed optimism or the demonstrated belief that you can do something, that there is reason to hope.**

STRATEGIES FOR UNSINKABLE OPTIMISM

Recognizing the world as a permanent whitewater world has a number of implications, not the least of which is that more than ever, you lead yourself. The sun may not shine on you. You may be wet and miserable. You may be battered and beaten. Like

Shackleton, you may find yourself stranded in the middle of nowhere. But this is no excuse for not being optimistic. Ask yourself: Are you having fun yet?

Create Optimism and Avoid Learned Helplessness

You can train yourself to be happy. As Benjamin Franklin said, "Do not anticipate trouble, or worry about what may not happen. Keep in the sunlight." Shackleton had plenty to worry about, *and* he took up the task at hand, keeping in the sunlight. Martin Seligman proposes specific techniques for "arguing" with ourselves to increase optimism and hope. This is the power of positive psychology and "learned optimism." Instead of dwelling on the daunting challenges ahead, taking an optimistic view can completely change the way you approach the challenge.

Seligman, building on the work of Aaron Beck, argues that how you think determines how you feel, and how you feel has everything to do with just about everything in your life: happiness, work, and love. He offers a number of approaches to amplify the positive and minimize the negative. He lays out a process for "arguing with one's self" when pessimistic: What's the evidence supporting your pessimism? What alternative explanations can you propose? What worst-case scenarios could result, and how likely are they, really? How useful is the pessimistic belief? The next step he terms "disputation" and involves the following actions: describing the adversity faced, labeling one's pessimistic beliefs, detailing the consequences of the beliefs, arguing against the beliefs, and mindfully noting one's internal affect as a result of the disputation. Learned optimism amounts to conscious, reality-based management of self in a world full of bumps and bruises.[2]

The flip side of learned optimism is "learned helplessness." Turbulent, permanent whitewater environments often lead to a feeling of being overwhelmed, a feeling of helplessness. This feeling, in and of itself, may cause paddlers to stop paddling at precisely the moment when they should be putting their heart and soul into it. You can collude with the "bad events" in your life—the failures. You can feel that what you do doesn't matter. You can become passive and pessimistic before the great roiling river. You can give up and drown. If Shackleton had met his adversities in this way, his entire party would likely have perished out there on the ice.

Such learned helplessness can have surprisingly far-reaching implications. Seligman and colleagues conducted studies with animals that experienced "learned helplessness." In one case, they were given shocks that they were unable to control. One of his graduate students, Madelon Visintainer, conducted an experiment with rats who were injected with cancer cells that would be expected to give half of them cancer under normal conditions. She placed one third of the rats in a control group. Another third was in a helpless situation where they were shocked without any way of preventing it. They learned helplessness. The last group of rats received shocks but could stop the shocks by pressing a bar. They were able to achieve mastery over the situation. In the control group, half the rats developed cancer, as expected. For the rats that had learned mastery (with the bar), only about 30 percent developed cancer. But for the rats that had learned helplessness, more than 70 percent developed cancer. While such studies cannot be explicitly replicated in humans, Seligman found similar effects in subsequent human research. Further, a series of studies suggest that optimistic people enjoy better health. Restated, pessimism kills. Most probably this holds even truer in whitewater environments, where he who is immobilized is lost.

We need to recognize that as a species we adapt well to environmental changes when we have to do so. Certainly, some people are less risk averse and find more enthusiasm for change. Some of us will engage in bungee jumping in our spare time, but many more will seek out a quiet cruise or weekend in a familiar seaside resort. Even those who choose risky activities such as sky diving or whitewater paddling exercise control. They would be less enthusiastic if someone had thrown them out of the plane or into the river without warning. Yet this is what happens in our organizations. The cheese keeps moving. Change comes unasked for, and it can easily prove as uncomfortable as a plunge into an icy river. This is how it is. But you need to find a way to take charge and not feel helpless. You need to cultivate optimism.

> Instead of dwelling on the daunting challenges ahead, taking an optimistic view can completely change the way you approach the challenge.

When All Else Fails, Paddle Like Hell

Sometimes you may commit to a certain course on the river and recognize that it is a mistake at the last minute. Too late! Even if you can see a better route, the water flows so fast that you have no choice but to proceed. In an organization, you may have a contract that locks you in. Maybe you have made commitments to others, and you don't want to let them down. You committed to do the job. The job has now changed, but you still feel like you made a commitment. And maybe you still have a mortgage to pay, car payments, and kids to keep in diapers. So you have to hang in there despite the terrifying look of the water ahead. You are committed. There is no way out of the situation but to go through it.

If this is the case, paddle like hell. A boat in motion is more stable than one bobbing aimlessly along the waves. The first reaction when you stare into the belly of the beast might be to freeze up. Paddlers sometimes call this the deer-in-the-headlights reaction, frozen with the paddle parallel to water, also known as the "pre-flip position." Don't do it. Put your paddle in the water. As with riding a bicycle, momentum, not braking, makes steering easier.

Keep your hands on the paddle and dig in. Pilots report that heavy reliance on automatic pilot systems diminishes their ability to spring into action should the situation require. Those who have their hands on the wheel are more engaged. They must pay more attention and keep more closely tuned to the situation and options before them. In flat water, if you are uncertain of your course, it is better to stop and take the time to analyze until you are more certain. In turbulent environments, stopping could be deadly. You need to act thoughtfully, but quickly.

> If you are committed to a certain course, you might have no choice but to go through it. If this is the case, paddle like hell. If you are mobile, you can continue to correct your trajectory more easily than if you freeze or dig in.

CHOOSE YOUR EQUIPMENT FOR THE RIGHT LEVEL OF FUN

Different people have different tolerances for play. There are many ways to go down a whitewater river, and they offer different levels of risk and fun. In general, if you define fun as excitement and adventure (not everyone does), the more risk you take, the greater the fun. If you paddle a play boat, you will play. If you paddle a more stable river runner, you may play a little less or a little differently. If you paddle in a raft, you will have many more limited opportunities to play but a relatively more stable existence.

Many organizational structures will work in this whitewater environment—from solo "company of one" enterprises to rafts that hold teams of people to flotillas of rafts that hold many people in flexible configurations to large motor launches that hold dozens of people in relative safety. We'll talk more about this in Chapter 8, "Building Flocks: Teaming for Today's Run," but your choice of vessel will determine the nature of your journey. In general, the more secure and stable the vessel, the fewer opportunities for fun. The huge motor launches that ply the Grand Canyon like buses are an exciting ride but a fairly secure one. They find little opportunity for independent exploration or personal risk of flipping or swimming.

If you do not care much for risk and play, then choose a vessel offering as much security as possible—perhaps a larger, more established organization. You can serve as a crew member in one of these teams and make a great contribution without having to stick your neck out as far. Of course, recognize that you are still in whitewater, so don't be surprised if you fall in. And don't be surprised, as happened to Rob on one of his first raft trips, if the captain is sucked out of the back of the raft, leaving you in charge.

If you can tolerate a bit more play and excitement in your life, then you can choose a riskier mode of work. Perhaps you join a start-up or go solo. The turbulence is greater, but you have more of a chance for play. You need to make this choice based on both your preferences and your skills. The choice, of course, will shape your experience. The skills you need for rafting differ from those used in kayaking. You can always switch later, but you will then, again, have to learn new skills. Take some time to think carefully about who you are and what you need, and how you can best balance your need for security and your need for play. The water will still run white, but you do have choices about how to run it.

> Your choice of vessel will determine the nature of your journey. If you want a more stable existence, work for a larger, more established organization. If you can handle a little more risk and play, join a start-up or go solo. Recognize, of course, that you are still in whitewater.

Patience: Keep Your Feet Up and Go With the Flow

Sometimes, patience proves a virtue. While you might need, on occasion, to "paddle like hell" to power through big water, once flipped and swimming, patience becomes a virtue. Know when to bide your time and let the river take its course. One of the mistakes paddlers who capsize make when they are swimming is instinctive: They try to stand in moving water. Their feet can then become wedged in a rock. Then, the current pushes the swimmer forward under the water. Even wearing a life jacket, the current can hold them under. Usually, rescuers can do little to help. People have drowned as a result of this dynamic. So paddlers in whitewater are advised to float through turbulence with their feet up and facing forward, as if they are sitting in a chair. Literally, they should "go with the flow."

If you find yourself in this situation, keep your feet (and your spirits) up. Don't lose heart. You will soon find a place where you can drag your soggy self out of the river into the sunlight. Exercise patience and float through the worst of the turbulence before trying to regain your footing. Don't become wedged in or locked in to a bad situation. You could well make matters worse.

In organizations, if you capsize in a turbulent situation, there are times when you have to float with the current for a while before it is safe to stand up and get out. Trying to exit or save yourself in the middle of the turbulence can make matters worse. There are times when you have to hold your breath and wait for the environment to settle down until you reach a point where you can rescue yourself. Maybe you have to have patience through a period of high stress at work or unemployment. These are periods when you might follow Winston Churchill's advice: "If you are going through hell…keep going."

If you attempt to paddle feverishly forever, then you will exhaust yourself. You might well do better to wait out the turbulence temporarily—for example, staying in your current organization even though it is challenging rather than jumping ship right away. If you can't stop it or step out of it, have patience and go with the flow.

> There are times when you have to float with the current, hold your breath and wait for the environment to settle down until you reach a point where you can rescue yourself. Keep your feet (and your spirits) up.

Recharge by Paddling

Pay attention to the "love quotient" of your life and work. Every job and every life has the tasks that you have to do to survive. You have to take out the garbage and show up on Monday after a weekend away. But you also need to have a percentage of your life and work that you love. Living or doing this percentage yields a direct, immediate, and often enduring energy. This percentage is your love quotient. Do more of what you love to do and the quotient rises. Do less, and it declines. Keep your love quotient high enough, and you will look forward to the day at hand and the day ahead. Let it fall too low, and the mere prospect of another day dampens your spirits and darkens your soul.

As a leader, the question becomes: What about your job do you truly love doing, so that the very doing of it energizes you? How much of your time do you spend doing what you love to do? Is that enough? If it isn't, then increase the percentage or risk burning out a valuable organizational and personal resource— yourself!

Certainly, healthy, intimate relationships in your personal life can increase the love in your life and bring both personal and professional joy and resilience. Such relationships require time, space, and energy (and a little luck) to develop. They are not transactions or tasks undertaken on the side without full attention or commitment. They provide another reason to tend to one's self outside work—in this case by giving yourself the time, space, and energy to grow love.

Attend to your emotional life and have connections outside work. Gallup has found that one predictor of *work* satisfaction and retention is to have a best friend at work, but this may not be the best thing for *life* satisfaction. This is especially true if you don't expect to be with the same company forever. It might be better advice to have at least two best friends, no more than one of whom is at work.

> Every job and every life has the
> tasks that you have to do to survive.
> You have to take out the garbage
> and show up on Monday after a
> weekend away. But you also have to
> have a percentage of your life
> and work that you love.

Create Time and Space for Play

To play, you need a playground. Jerry Hirshberg, describing the Nissan Design Institute, stresses the importance of providing time and space in organizations for play. The highly skilled and dedicated designers at a prominent international firm still struggled against ossification…and they were professional, career inventors. They were masters of play![3]

Hirshberg advocates hiring (and then managing) divergent pairs to create abrasion that will blur the boundaries of our thinking. The abrasion sparks play and creativity, makes planning more porous, and pushes more deeply informed decision making. And when the designers were mentally stuck or emotionally stymied? Shut down the institute and go to a movie (literally). Do something to reenergize yourself, your relationships, and your work.

Jack Kennedy knew this. As the story goes, young Senator Kennedy participated in a particularly stressful and prolonged meeting in Boston. Tensions ran high as did the stakes. Nerves frayed and a resolution seemed unlikely. At one point, Kennedy's staff looked around and said, "Where's Jack?" No one had seen him leave. A combination of concern for his well-being and resentment for being abandoned fueled an unsuccessful search of the premises for their leader. A longtime aide and friend knew where to look. He went to the nearest Bailey's Ice Cream Parlor. Sure enough, there sat the senator from Massachusetts, alone with his very own Bailey's ice cream sundae. The aide knew what Jack knew: The answer did not lie in the room. This was not a time to paddle harder; this was a time to play.

Play is also good for your health. As Daniel Pink writes, "Ample evidence points to the enormous health and professional benefits of laughter, lightheartedness, games, and humor...too much sobriety can be bad for your career and worse for your general well-being...in work and in life, we all need to play."[4] George Vaillant offers the following advice for "aging well" based on studies of the aging process: Stay engaged with people and ideas, tolerate "cheerfully...the indignities of old age," maintain hope with as much independence and initiative as physically possible, laugh and play, enjoy the view backward and forward, and honor your friends even as you look for new ones.[5] As Betty Friedan once said, "the exercise of our unique human capacity for mindful control is key to vital age versus decline."[6]

> **Play is good for your health. When you find yourself mentally stuck or emotionally stymied, do something to reenergize yourself, your relationships, and your work.**

CULTIVATE EXUBERANCE

Permanent whitewater requires not only a positive spirit, but what Kay Redfield Jamison calls "exuberance." Teddy Roosevelt bore nearly daily testimony to such passionate spirit and its power, from riding with his Rough Riders to creating national parks to exploring the Amazon. It appears also in the persistent intensity of Wilson "Snowflake" Bentley, a Vermont farmer whose passion for photographing snowflakes made him the world's foremost authority. Jamison writes, "Exuberance carries us to places we would not otherwise go—across the savannah, to the moon, into the imagination.... I believe that exuberance is incomparably more important than we acknowledge.... Exuberant people take in the world and act upon it differently than those who are less lively and energetically engaged."[7]

If you are not naturally exuberant, and not all of us are, try to connect with exuberance. Jamison points out that exuberance can be contagious, as seen in leaders with "infectious enthusiasm." Such exuberance can lead to unnecessary risks, but consider the words of Katharine Graham, legendary publisher and CEO of *The Washington Post*, "I loved my job, I loved the paper, I loved the whole company."[8] Such exuberance gives you the fortitude to meet difficult challenges and the momentum for achievement. A whitewater environment has tremendous force and danger. You need to meet it with equal force. Don't wait for it to happen to you. Grab your paddle and plunge in. Find the fun. Optimism and exuberance can turn serious challenges into opportunities for play and threatening whitewater into an exhilarating run.

> A whitewater environment has tremendous force and danger. You need to meet it with equal force. Don't wait for it to happen to you. Grab your paddle and plunge in. Find the fun.

 THE TAKEOUT

Meeting a turbulent environment with optimism and a sense of play can make the difference between a frightening ride and a fully engaging adventure.

CHAPTER 5

Personal Flotation
You Are Responsible for Your Own Security

> *The explorer... is looking, not for thrills, but for facts about the unknown.... To him, an adventure is merely a bit of bad planning, brought to light by the test of trial.... Serious work in exploration calls for as definite and rigorous professional preparation as does success in any other serious work in life.*[1]
>
> —Roald Amundsen, Polar Explorer

At 36, Kathleen Flinn was laid off from her secure corporate job with Microsoft in London. She walked out of the office in December 2003 with all her belongings in a box. The layoff shocked her. They had thrown her out of her warm cubicle into the cold water. She thought about joining her boyfriend in Seattle, but he urged her to go to Paris to pursue her lifelong dream of becoming a chef. Cooking and restaurants had always fascinated Flinn. In fact, she had handled the restaurant section of MSN's online city guides before it was sold to Citysearch. She enrolled in the famous Le Cordon Bleu restaurant school in Paris, became a chef, and wrote about her experiences in her memoir, *The Sharper Your Knife, the Less You Cry: Love, Laughter, and Tears at the World's Most Famous Cooking School.*[2]

The vessel carrying her work life capsized, but she found a way to rescue herself. In fact, she thought creatively about her career and used her layoff as an opportunity to pursue her passions for cooking and writing. She didn't drown. Far from it. She paddled off into the sunset. Others might not make such a dramatic shift. Perhaps they could find a similar position in a new organization or use the opportunity to pursue additional education in their current field. Regardless, having the mindset and the skills to recover when your boat capsizes matters most. Because in whitewater, your boat, almost certainly, will flip.

Managers who recognize this reality may actually throw their employees into the water. One upper-middle manager at a large, national communications company found that to retain good employees, he had to *encourage* them to look for other jobs. Had he lost his mind? But look at his problem. A white-hot labor market fed by tremendous industry growth had taken 3 of his 11 managerial direct reports from his company in the previous 18 months. More than a quarter of his staff was gone. By the time he found out about their departures, it usually was too late to do anything. Competitors recruited openly in his parking lot before work, during lunch, and after work. Of course, he returned the favor, but churning people or outright losing them hurt his operation. Turnover of supervisory and managerial personnel unnecessarily and unproductively disrupted the world of the 120 staff members they led.

If the manager kept doing what he was doing, the future looked like more of the same—trying to hold his crew together amidst a pell-mell race down the rapids of expansion. He needed to do something about this swirling, roiling job market. So he turned his thinking on its head: To keep employees, encourage exploration. He *required* that his direct reports schedule one or more external job interviews every three months and to *discuss* at least one of these interviews with him. Certainly, they could explore more than one possibility, and there might be some they didn't choose to share, but every quarter they had to go on a job interview and discuss it with him. He cut them loose in their own boats to keep them with his own expedition.

Is this any way for a manager to lead—encouraging his people to look for new jobs? What was he thinking? There was a method to his madness. First, if everyone ultimately serves as his or her own boss, navigating his or her own career kayak, then people should plunge into the river, and he should be out there with them. More specifically, they should take a look around for themselves, and he should know what they see, what they discover. The benefits? His people would gain more awareness of the broader world, and he would learn what they were thinking and what they wanted. He could speak to them before they had an offer in hand and were headed out the door. He could keep his best people rather than being left with, in his words, "only the unconscious or RIPs (retired in place)." He would also learn about how he was doing as a leader. He wanted people to choose actively and regularly to work with him. He wanted the energy such choice liberates.

He didn't try to fight the turbulence of job churn. It was going to go on whether he acknowledged it or not. Instead, he turned his thinking on its head to navigate better this turbulence by moving with it.

He instituted his policy. It was crazy, upside down thinking. He held his meetings with staff. He improved his knowledge of the job market. He learned more about his direct reports. He grew in his understanding of his work relations with each of his direct reports. Over the next 18 months, the job market continued to roil. And here is the really surprising thing: Only one of his direct reports left his company. Just one. This turns conventional thinking about employee retention on its head. To keep good people, you have to be willing to give them away. You don't handcuff them to their rowing stations; you throw them into the water.

And even if you don't have an enlightened boss encouraging you to do this, shouldn't you test the waters on your own?

> One upper-middle manager at a large, national communications company found that to retain good employees, he had to *encourage* them to look for other jobs.

 DON'T LEAVE SHORE WITHOUT IT

Once when Rob was paddling on the New River in West Virginia, a young girl was swept through one of the rapids without a life jacket. The teenager had been swimming with friends in the pool at the top of Fayette Station rapid just below the famous New River Gorge Bridge, the world's largest steel-span bridge. She got too close to the top and was swept into the Class IV rapid, without a boat and without a personal flotation device (PFD). She gasped for air as the river pulled her over rocks. She bobbed up and then was dragged through holes. She surfaced and then was drawn down under waves.

When she arrived at the bottom of the rapids, she was still alive, but barely. She did not have the strength to swim to shore. As she went down for the last time, an alert kayaker raced out and pulled her onto the deck of his boat. He paddled her to shore. She was white as a sheet, but miraculously survived. It was a lesson in the power and danger of being unprepared in such an unforgiving environment. In this environment, you need to have your own personal flotation, and to take responsibility for your own security.

Safety begins with the right equipment, such as personal flotation, a helmet, and shoes. A whistle can help draw attention in an emergency and a knife can help cut free a paddler who becomes entangled. In cold weather conditions, a paddle jacket, a wetsuit, or polypropylene (not cotton) clothing are essential gear for avoiding hypothermia.

In an organization, your PFD comes in the form of a portfolio of experience, a strong personal and professional network for support, and an ability to live with and manage change. A portfolio of experience will allow you to find a new role if your job capsizes. A network of support, personal and professional, will help pull you from the river *before* the hypothermia sets in. And the ability to live with and manage change will allow you to look for opportunities to save yourself. Thrown into the turbulent waters of organizational life, these could save your life.

SINK OR SWIM

On the ocean liner, security came from being part of the crew that kept the ship afloat. The ship was designed to withstand wind and wave and was kept on course through the ability and discipline of a large and specialized crew. As long as the overall organization succeeded, your position as a sailor was secure. In that environment, workers joined a large, stable organization and stayed for life. But, the paddler in whitewater cannot look to the organization for security.

Security in permanent whitewater is personal. It depends on personal skills and personal mindset. Many people could perhaps throw you a rescue line, but in the end your security is in your own hands. Once upon a time, people identified themselves by where they worked: "Hi, my name is Mary, and I'm a manager at C-Corp." Today, people identify themselves by what they do: "Hi, my name is Mary, and I'm an account manager." This change represents a shift away from people identifying themselves with a mother ship to defining themselves in terms of what they do. This change reflects an awareness of the basic change in the workplace spawned initially by the brutal downsizing of the 1980s: You are on your own.

Correspondingly, we should think about work not as a formal job but rather as a portfolio of projects that require a particular set of skills. The labor market will value those skills, especially those related to temporary, project-based work. A job interviewer will quickly move past titles held to tasks performed. Can you give evidence of flexibility? Of "down field" thinking? Of moving in and out of temporary teaming arrangements? Of working independently and yet collaboratively? Of negotiating new work relations? Of maintaining a strong network over time? The question is not where you have worked, but what can you do?

> We should think about work not as a formal job but rather as a portfolio of projects that require a particular set of skills. The question is not where you have worked, but what can you do?

STRATEGIES FOR PERSONAL FLOTATION

How do you take responsibility for your own safety? The following sections explore a number of strategies for protecting yourself and creating your own flotation in the face of turbulence.

Learn Self-Rescue by Developing Your "Brand You"

Pressures to downsize, rightsize, and resize have shredded many organizations. Global opportunities and challenges kept organizations churning even amidst periods of the highest growth. Nearly three decades of whitewater have atomized labor markets and the organizations that depend on them. The "Brand Called You" phenomenon sprang from the 1980s and now thrives in physical space as well as cyberspace. Employees learned under imposed duress and now actively leverage this truth: They are on their own. Furthermore, they are what they do or can do, not where, for whom, or even under what title they did it. The opportunity and threat of "going it alone" down the river or, perhaps more accurately, of going from temporary kayaking group to temporary kayaking group means that you are your own brand, your own certified promise of what you can do. The certification comes from your track record and from your fellow travellers. Others organizing a trip need to know what they can and cannot count on from you.[3]

So-called "free agents" account for about 30 percent of the American workforce.[4] In 2007, 33 percent of workers in Japan, supposedly a bastion of ocean liner security and lifetime employment, qualified as "nonregular" workers. The size and prominence of Manpower, Inc. bears witness to the temporary nature of employment: 4,400 offices in 73 countries and territories; $17.6 billion in revenue in 2006 (85 percent outside the United States); 400,000 customers worldwide, including all the Fortune 100 and 98 percent of the Fortune 500 companies; 30,000 staff; and 4.4 million placements in 2006. (Pause and take that in: 4.4 million placements in one year! Manpower leads a small nation of temp workers.)[5] And Manpower is just one of the companies providing this service.

Daniel Pink, author of *Free Agent Nation: The Future of Working for Yourself*, says the changing workplace looks increasingly like present day Hollywood—and not just because of the intensity of the drama. "Large permanent organizations with fixed rosters of individuals are giving way to small, flexible networks with ever-changing collections of talent."[6] How strong is your "Brand You?" If you didn't have your corporation and title on your business card, what would you have? To star in your own film you need flexible networks. What can you do to strengthen your brand?

> ## So-called "free agents" account for about 30 percent of the American workforce.

Build a Portfolio of Projects

People don't have jobs anymore. They have portfolios of projects. This differs from mid- to late-twentieth century, when a worker peg fit more neatly into a position, and the "organization man" held sway. Working successfully on projects requires strong emotional intelligence and adept use of stakeholder mapping. Master a project management software (ideally in combination with a transparent groupware). Go to a workshop on teams, decision-making, and running meetings.[7] Learn responsibility charting, a method of pairing key project steps with stakeholder analysis and then employing its language to categorize decision-making roles. These techniques enable you to put a far sharper edge on "who is doing what when" than can standard job descriptions.[8] Less formal and up-to-date role definition places more importance on you defining them.

Above all, recognize that each project amounts to a run down the river. Temporary teams assemble with a wide range of possible interdependence, as discussed in Chapter 8, "Building Flocks:

Teaming for Today's Run." This means that everything—everything—is at least potentially a negotiation. Negotiation and its sister skill persuasion should figure prominently in your tool box, aka, your survival kit. Attend a negotiation workshop or two or three.[9] Finally, practice, practice, practice, at work, at home, and in the world at large.

> **People don't have jobs anymore.**
> **They have portfolios of projects.**

Practice Your Offside Roll: Cultivate Diverse Skills to Increase Maneuverability

In kayaking, you need to practice an offside roll. If you typically roll on the right side, you need to do some practice rolling on the left and vice versa. Then, should you find yourself in a situation where you cannot make your onside roll, you have another option. For example, you might be stuck in a hydraulic (pinned in the current like a piece of wood in the backwash at the bottom of a waterfall) in a way that makes it impossible to set up on your onside. At this point, experienced kayakers will switch hands while they are underwater and try a roll on the other side. It will sometimes do the trick. Practicing offside also increases skill level, confidence, and the ability to meet unexpected challenges.

In work, you might cultivate a set of other skills so that you have a fallback career if your first one takes a turn for the worse or ceases to be engaging. When Kathleen Flinn's corporate job dumped her unceremoniously into the brink, she leveraged her passion for cooking and writing to start afresh. Play in other areas may keep your primary career more interesting, or it could become the primary career. Try something completely different. Bruce McEwen, author of *The End of Stress as We Know It*, says the key to beating stress is to plunge into short-term projects that are different from your typical work.[10] Discussing the current understanding of stress, he delineates the physiological consequences of stress and the rise of stressors—simply stated, while we have more access to the basics that so occupied (preoccupied) our ancestors, our permanent whitewater generates ever more stressors. Successfully addressing stress turns on "plunging into a short-lived program that bears little resemblance to one's life but by gradually and permanently building in new habits based on an understanding of how brain and body work."[11]

In the process we wire and rewire our brains and our bodies. We increase our behavioral, psychological, and emotional repertoire for dealing with the range of contemplated and unimagined challenges that a permanent whitewater environment can hurl at us. Or, as McEwen says, "remember the evidence that by repeated thoughts and actions we can alter not only the functioning but also the structure of the neural networks in our brains."[12] Training and skill development help us increase our sense of control and build a set of diverse skills that might come in handy downstream.

In whitewater, security comes from maneuverability. The boat has no keel and no rudder. Stability comes from the ability to move quickly, change direction, and stay afloat. Paddlers learn strokes such as the sweep and draw to turn their boats quickly, and learn to brace themselves to respond to turbulence. Your feet do not rest on a solid deck.

When you leave the crew of the ocean liner, you have to give up the illusion of control and the desire for stability. You no longer look out for the occasional iceberg. You pick your way around rocks and through waves. The more maneuverable you can make your thinking and the more varied your skills, the greater your stability.

As you work, you should develop skills for the challenges you will likely face in the future. Consider Harry Houdini, the master escape artist. He devised his own tricks, but he knew that he could not control all the risks, hence he kept perfecting his skills. He not only practiced breaking out of handcuffs and straitjackets, but he also prepared himself for hostile environments. For example, when he prepared for some winter escapes in a river, he took successively colder baths each day to condition his body to the shock of cold water, and he worked on improving his ability to hold his breath. He didn't know exactly how he would use this unusual set of skills, but it certainly seemed like they might prove useful given his line of work.

Once, this conditioning came in particularly handy. He was lowered through the hole in an icy river and he escaped from his bonds quickly. Yet, he could not find the hole in the ice. People on the shore waited. The minutes passed. Where was he? Had he perished? He was still alive, stealing breaths from the air pockets under the ice as he searched for the exit. He found the hole and emerged safely. His conditioning in anticipation of known and unknown challenges had saved him. Surviving under the ice is not a skill that everyone will need, but something akin to it belongs in your portfolio. Consider what you might face downriver. Consider what you actually have in your portfolio of skills. Look at the river ahead with a clear eye and, if necessary, start filling up the bathtub with ice.

Our distant ancestors emerged from the oceans with bodies largely composed of salt water. In effect, they carried their environment with them. We now adapt ourselves to live on all seven continents, on mountains, under the sea, and above the sky. Part of this adaptation comes from the relatively forgiving nature of our physiology, but much of it comes from our ability to create familiar environmental pockets through shells such as tents, planes, submarines, ocean liners, kayaks, and spacecraft. We continue to evolve the main engine of that adaptability, namely our brain.[13] In our lives, we also create psychological and emotional shells to build our sense of security—degrees, career paths, and titles.

Organizational change often entails altering these shells. You might need to adopt new equipment with more flexibility and maneuverability, equipment better suited to this environment. Like a hermit crab, you sometimes have to change your shell. Do you occupy the right shell for a permanent whitewater environment?

A good defense can be the best offense in meeting change. While a life jacket and helmet are important on the river, paddling skills can keep you from needing to use your life jacket or paddling past the point of no return. A skilled and alert driver could make an airbag unnecessary. A skilled trapeze artist will never have to test the net (although it is nice to know it is there). In organizations, the value of your own skills affords you true security. If your current organization values your skills, then you will continue to have a position there. If other organizations value your skills, then you will have opportunities to find work with them. In addition to specific skills, you need the broader skills in managing change as described in this book. Above all, you need the mindset to keep identifying and developing key skills.

> In whitewater, security comes from maneuverability. Cultivate a set of other skills so that you have a fallback career if your first one takes a turn for the worse or ceases to engage you.

SWEEPING AND TURNING

In the sweep stroke, the kayaker moves the paddle from front to rear with a sweep out to the side, turning the bow of the boat in the opposite direction. This is just one of many steering strokes that you can apply in forward and reverse directions to turn quickly to correct course in the midst of turbulent water. In organizational and market whitewater, the more you can increase your maneuverability, the more easily you can get out of harm's way or seize temporary opportunities. Part of keeping yourself safe is to learn to maneuver more quickly and more effectively.

At work, maneuverability is vital to continued success. Build people skills that are transferable to other jobs. Think carefully about investing time in learning company-specific or technology-specific skills, since both will likely change. Occasionally, you will need to invest in learning something very idiosyncratic and localized—but be aware of how this might reduce your future flexibility. Think about how each assignment prepares you for a new role at your current company or at a new one. Ensure that you concentrate on developing flexible and transferable skill sets so that you create and re-create the power to sweep and turn throughout your career.

Much of the business self-development literature focuses on the importance of ongoing development, of refining existing skills and developing new ones.[14] Keep learning. Practice your offside roll. Make a commitment to ongoing personal and professional development.

Create Strong Networks

Even while your safety depends primarily on your own actions, you are not entirely alone on the river. You might still look to others for safety. To think like a paddler is to avoid taking a strictly "Me, Inc." view of the world. You paddle with others and depend on them for the work you do and for safety. One can argue that in many ways you depend more on others now than ever before even as you depend on yourself more than ever before. Welcome to another paradox of permanent whitewater. (We'll consider this "safety in numbers" a bit more in Chapter 8 on teaming.)

Collegial cooperation can significantly increase the odds for successful navigation of dangerous turns in the river. Even in the Rolodex age, networks were critical.[15] In the greater turbulence and faster pace of the MySpace and BlackBerry era, the power of a personal network only becomes more important. Networks such as LinkedIn span organizations and keep you connected with friends and professional colleagues in other organizations. These networks, as well as less digital ones—for example, networks around church or school or local community—can offer valuable resources and connections when the ocean liner breaks apart. Their members can help to keep hard times at bay and come to your rescue when hard times arrive. They provide leads and certify your abilities.

What do these network members look for? First and foremost, reliability counts. Peers especially pay attention to whether you do what you say you will do. Decades of research on corporate high potentials has documented this seemingly obvious point. And if that mattered 20, 30, or 40 years ago in a more structured and stable time, then it matters even more in our whitewater times. Time is short and the river demanding. "Anyone know someone who can help with…?"

Networks matter more than ever, but when push comes to shove, you are responsible for your own safety. You will need to rely first and foremost on your own skills and equipment for your survival. Make sure your own life jacket is zipped up, your helmet is tight, and your spray skirt secure.

> One can argue that in many ways you depend more on others now than ever before even as you depend on yourself more than ever before. Welcome to another paradox of permanent whitewater.

Take Care of Your Health

As noted in Chapter 2, "Working the Eddies: Pace Yourself to Preserve Your Sanity," pacing is vital to building in breaks in a relentless and unpredictable environment. You also need to watch your health. Get yourself a decent health plan—it's worth the money. Get regular checkups. Utilize specialists. Subscribe to a medical newsletter (Harvard has one; Mayo has one) or visit WebMD regularly. Pay particular attention to articles about lifestyle—exercise, relaxation, and food. Food matters—in the short run and for the long haul. If world-class athletes regularly refine their routines, diets, medical care, and psychological practices, then why not you? They play their game intermittently. You play yours every day.

We need to get tough. Medical evidence suggests that rising allergy rates in the United States might be because kids don't play in the dirt enough. They are not exposed to an environment that allows the immune system to get stronger. Researchers have even found that working in the dirt can help alleviate depression because microorganisms in dirt appear to activate serotonin production.[16] So if someone tells you "go pound dirt" or even to "eat dirt," thank them for the advice—and take it. You need to put yourself in situations that will test and develop your immune system…literally and metaphorically.

> You also need to watch your health.
> If world-class athletes regularly
> refine their routines, diets, medical
> care, and psychological practices,
> then why not you? They play
> their game intermittently.
> You play yours every day.

ALONE IN A TIGHT PLACE

Years ago, Rob's father was once swallowed alive on the "Top Yough." He was kayaking through a Class V rapid on the perilous upper section of Youghiogheny River in Western Pennsylvania. It was at a rapid called "Suckhole," so named because a huge boulder with a triangular hole like an open drain gulped down about 60 percent of the river and anything that happened to be floating in it. The water ran under the rock—an undercut rock—one of the most dangerous hazards on a river.

He made a wrong turn and was sucked down this drain, boat and all. Out of his boat and under the rock, the river swept him into a dark tunnel and to what looked like certain doom. He grabbed a little air from a pocket under the rock. He figured he might have a 50/50 chance of washing out the other side alive if he conserved his air. After what seemed like an eternity, he astonishingly popped up in a hidden air chamber in the heart of the rock. One thing was certain under that rock, he was on his own. He alone was responsible for his own survival.

The bow of his boat emerged from the depths and jabbed him in the chest. He pushed it down, and it disappeared deep beneath the rock. It showed him that there was a channel down there somewhere. But to follow the boat he would have to take off his life jacket and swim under the rock, hoping that his air held out and he didn't get snagged in the channel on his way out. It was not a very attractive proposition. Then he looked up and saw a sliver of light above his head. There was a narrow crack in the rock. He stripped off his life jacket and just barely squeezed through the crack.

As the minutes ticked by, his fellow paddlers on the outside feared the worst. There was nothing they could do. After five minutes under the rock, they had given up hope that they would see him alive. They could do nothing. But then they saw him wave his hand through the crack in the rock.

In a turbulent environment, you cannot expect someone to come and save you. This is the reality of whitewater. The team around you will help you when they can (and you will help them), but not when you are under several tons of rock. Then, you carry responsibility for your own security. You have to find your own way.

Are you building the skills today that you will need when you find yourself in such a tight space? Are you prepared to take charge if your career capsizes? Do you have an offside roll? Do you have the maneuverability to avoid peril? Do you have the right flotation to keep your head above water? What skills and equipment will you need to survive downstream and how can you build them? Remember, you are responsible for your own safety.

 THE TAKEOUT

You can't depend on the ocean liner for security; you have to stand ready to rescue yourself.

CHAPTER 6

Scouting and Portaging
Set Your Own Course

*Few other sports require the processing of so much data so
fast. Survival depends on split-second decisions, both reflexive
and deliberate—and not just one or two in a drop, but continuously, in a dynamic flow of constant recalibration. One
mistake in the thousands of moves in a single day—going a
foot too far to the left, or getting thumped off line at the wrong
moment—and your life may end.*[1]
—Peter Heller, Outside magazine, on the descent
of Tibet's Upper Tsangpo Gorge

On the tenth day of an historic first run down the menacing
Upper Tsangpo Gorge in Tibet in 2002, kayaker Johnnie Kern
was driving into a "must-make" ferry—paddling upstream across
the current to a safe haven behind a rock. Two other paddlers had
made it safely into the eddy behind the rock. But a wave curling
off the eddy pushed Kern back into the current. He was flipped
and plunged down the Class V rapid. In the same rapid, his teammate, Steve Fisher was swallowed by a huge hole and rolled up
holding his paddle in two pieces. Using half his paddle like a
canoer, he battled his way through another large hole to the
bottom.[2]

The paddlers all arrived safely at the bottom, but they took very different routes. They had run the same rapid but had had completely different experiences. They scouted the rapids from the shore and chose routes, but each one had to read the water and react in real time to make his own way downstream. In whitewater, you have to read the water and make sense of the environment around you, overall as well as minute by minute, even instant by instant.

When the Tsangpo expedition reached Rainbow Falls four days later, they had made history as the first team to run the Upper Gorge and survive. This was a river 20 times steeper than the Colorado through the Grand Canyon. To avoid a suicidal run during monsoon runoff, they made the run in winter, paddling through icy waters and trudging through Himalayan snows. At several points along the way, they assessed that the water was simply too dangerous to run, and they chose to portage. At Rainbow Falls, they made a 96-hour portage above the falls and through a 12,000-foot pass, a trek never before attempted in winter. The only thing more dangerous or difficult would have been running the river itself at this point. When they reached the Lower Gorge, they realized floods had washed away the rocky bank up to the 300-foot cliffs, making it impossible to scout. Expedition leader Scott Lindgren determined that it was too dangerous to attempt these unknown rapids without scouting and without the opportunity for portaging. In this case, discretion proved the better part of valor. They hiked out and ended the journey. It would have been crazy to continue.

An ocean liner has the luxury of charting a clear course from Point A to Point B. The captain spreads out the maps and decides on the course. Heading set, the crew shares a vision and works together to maintain the course. The captain plans, and the crew executes. Planning in whitewater, on the other hand, emerges. Every paddle stroke depends on the one that came before. There is no absolute truth. Meaning is local. The grand direction may not come down from the captain. Instead, there are directional statements: We are all headed downstream—into the unknown. You need the ability to read the water for yourself and to recognize the sound of dangers, to know when to pause to rest, stop to think, or pull out and portage.

> In whitewater, you have to read the water and make sense of the environment around you, overall as well as minute by minute, even instant by instant.

MEANING IS LOCAL

If ever there was an ocean liner, it was the power industry in the United States during most of the twentieth century. Fifty separate, state-run monopolies oversaw the generation, transmission, and distribution of power. They were stable, community-based, engineering-dominated organizations. Doing one's job meant keeping one's job, a predictable schedule, and a decent income. The occasional, often weather-related emergency led to an activity spike. Employees pulled together to overcome adversity to restore electrical service to their community. The fact that often 10 or 15 percent of a power company's employees were related to one another bore witness to the overall appeal of the work and the life that went with it.

Deregulation brought dramatic changes: new stakeholders and competitors as well as conflicting market pressures and shareholder demands. At one power company, the COO watched as a series of "snap" surveys revealed steadily declining employee morale. Corridor buzz revealed the main cause to any who would listen: fear of being sold. The fear was well founded: Deregulation predictably leads to consolidation of human and financial capital—restated, fewer players, fewer jobs.

The COO decided that he needed to act. He added a tour of facilities to his activities, traveling to every location and talking to virtually all employees in a series of small, 30-minute meetings. He showed them a simple set of four numbers—their current cost per kilowatt hour of generating electricity, the cost of production of their cheapest regional competitor, the numbers for the best performer in the United States, and projections for declining energy production prices over the next three to five years. Their cost was the highest, and this was the real concern. All of them faced this new permanent whitewater reality and its potentially chilling consequences.

The COO told them the game now played was cutting costs without sacrificing reliability. If they could do that, then they might reduce the chance of the company being sold. Or if it was sold, the acquirer would more likely look to buy their best practices and not to gut the organization. He showed them the river. He told them about the whitewater downstream. Then, he asked them whether they wanted to stay and work with him to meet this challenge. Further, he advised them that if they did not wish to do so, then they should leave not just the organization but the industry—now.

He told them that he understood their concerns about the company being sold. He went on to tell them that they were worried about the wrong thing: They needed to worry about the changing nature of the game, of the water they were traveling. The logo on their chest did not matter; being sold did not matter. What mattered was how well they could play this new business game, a game that few if any in the room had signed up to play. They had not signed up. Their relatives had not signed up. Their community had not signed up. The company, which had enjoyed a fairly stable environment for generations, had now plunged into permanent whitewater. He told them that the river is what the river is, and they needed to focus on the new realities of the industry and master the mindset and skills required.

In the past, he might have told the employees, so many of them detail-hungry engineers, exactly where the company expected to be in 10 years and what he expected them to do to help get there. He could have shown them countless PowerPoint slides analyzing their world, laying out a detailed plan—a specific endpoint. He would wrap it all up in a neat package. He would set the course, and they would execute against the plan. But time—a short time—would have demonstrated the plan wrong. Such detail might have provided employees a greater sense of security in the moment, albeit a short moment before they saw the flaws and the mounting gap between the original plan, however inspired, and a rapidly changing reality. Then, the fleeting moment of security would end and leadership's credibility would fall. Fear and perhaps panic would come into view.

These current meetings reflected a new and different time. The meetings captured and symbolized a fundamental environmental change. In this deregulated world, the COO didn't tell the employees exactly where they were headed. He didn't know. The COO told them, in essence, that no one had figured out how to play this new game. Figuring out the nature of the game, this permanent whitewater game, had proved difficult enough. People needed help with their mindsets, forget the details of a plan. The COO, an engineer himself, understood that. He stopped, scouted the river, and reported back. He did not want his people to find themselves drifting, either assuredly or anxiously, and then floundering in uncertainty in the middle of the river. He did not want them either to feel betrayed as they went under (or out) with a curse against the COO on their lips. Neither did he want them to feel alone, abandoned, and scared. He wanted them to know what lay ahead and to make a personal call about how best to proceed downstream. He wanted his people to see what he saw:

an ongoing challenge of a different nature and a pressing need to develop new skills throughout the organization, skills in reading the river and in making one's way through permanent whitewater.

He didn't pretend to have specific answers, only a strategic understanding of what lay ahead and where they all needed to focus. The numbers were all approximations, crude approximations. He sought to deliver truth and guidance, not precision. He was telling them they were facing Class IV and V rapids, and this was the way down a very long, perhaps endless, river. He didn't try to describe every rapid along the way in detail because the detail would change and none of this would make any sense until they got into the water. He showed them the channel and identified the rocks. He told them what it would take to succeed (and he provided the training and resources). Then, he asked: Are you going on with me or pulling out?

Equally important, the COO had demonstrated a key skill in navigating the permanent whitewater they now faced. He did not simply collect and transmit information. No, he scouted. He understood the consequences of what he saw. He conveyed meaning. A good scout does not simply go and look. A good scout goes and sees, and then connects the dots. Good data and even better information comes from a good scout. A good scout creates meaning from an otherwise unknown or poorly understood environment. In that, the scout provides directional truth and guidance, a way to proceed and the key reasons to do so.

The COO finished his tour of the organization, meeting with well over 90 percent of employees in these small group sessions. Several weeks after this series of meetings the company sampled morale among workers. It was higher than when the slide in morale began. He hadn't given them answers. But he had given them a frame of reference for making their own sense of the environment. Some people left, but most stayed and, stay or go, they all knew in general terms what they faced. Most importantly, those who stayed were ready to take it on.

> He was telling them this was the
> way down a very long, perhaps
> endless, river. He didn't try to
> describe every rapid along the way
> in detail. He told them what it would
> take to succeed. Then, he asked:
> Are you going on with me
> or pulling out?

GET OUT WHEN YOU HEAR THE ROAR OF THE FALLS

As the COO and the members of the Tsangpo Gorge expedition realized, you need to recognize when your read of the water indicates that it is not safe to proceed. Reaching a large waterfall is such a point. The equivalent of a waterfall in an organization is a situation in which your sanity or your physical health and safety are threatened. Going on could mean emotional or even physical death. That said, it is never an easy decision to pull out of the stream. You lose the momentum and buoyancy of travel on the river. You derail your career. You end friendships. You give up much, including some or all of your gear, perhaps even treasured pieces. The path around the falls will undoubtedly prove arduous and present its own difficulties. At times, you think taking your chances going downstream would have been better. But, when you hear the sound of the falls, the only way forward is out.

A manager in his early forties came to an executive education program in the midst of a successful career as a turnaround artist. Clearly, from the day that he walked into the classroom, he was not a happy camper. What he did for a living was only slightly more pleasant than the job of executioner. He had spent most of the previous decade as the "boots on the ground" for those buying companies to flip them. He ripped them apart and moved on. He was very good at it, but he had also developed deep misgivings. It was killing him.

He knew this when he walked into the one-week program. He worked through the exercises about leading change and identifying a personal vision and mission. He gained a crystalline clarity that he did not want to go further down this river. By the end of the week, he had made his decision. He realized that he had become very good at doing something that he didn't like to do. He decided to go back on Monday morning and quit his job. He realized that he wanted to work instead in social action in the nonprofit sector, something he had done two decades earlier when in his twenties. Now it was the 1990s and social action had fallen out of favor. He was by no means choosing a simple course. This would entail long hours with little pay. It would mean committing to outcomes that would prove extremely difficult to measure. He knew, though, that saving himself required getting off this river. Any other choice would amount to sailing over the falls. He had to portage.

Our early forties often provide the occasion for this type of reassessment. Generally speaking, in your twenties, you try many things. In your thirties, you become very good at a few things and are rewarded for doing them well. By your forties, you more likely find yourself frequently considering what to do with your acquired skills. In your fifties, helping others to choose and develop grows more prominent.

Any developmental stage can trigger a portage or even several. The prompt may come from within one's self or from the organization. You may come to see the mix of your life as needing much more or less of this or that ingredient, or you may experience your organization as increasingly unfulfilling, perhaps dysfunctional or even toxic.

Your physical health may trigger a portage. Your body may tell you that you need a change. As press secretary for then Vice President George H. W. Bush, Peter Teeley was at the center of power inside the Beltway when he was diagnosed with colon cancer in 1991 at the age of 51. He underwent surgery and chemotherapy. He also quit his job in Washington and was sworn in as Ambassador to Canada in 1992, arguably the quietest of political appointments. Teeley spent a blissful year out of the turbulent river of Washington life before Bill Clinton came to office, and he dove back into the river as a corporate executive for Amgen. Teeley recovered from his cancer and wrote about his experiences 15 years later.[3] In this case, an internal threat led to the portage. Sometimes the health threat can be more direct: As in, the job itself is hazardous to your health. If the river runs you and you lack the option to adjust your pace as discussed in Chapter 2, "Working the Eddies: Pace Yourself to Preserve Your Sanity," then portage.

Sometimes it is not the absolute level of the river—a waterfall—but rather a mismatch between level and skill. A paddler took a few years off from kayaking. He came back to the Tohickon, a Class III/IV river in Eastern Pennsylvania. In the years that he was away from paddling, he had lost his Eskimo roll. He hit the first rapid and swam. Fellow travelers fished him out and he started down river again. He hit another drop and swam again. Then he swam again. And again. By about the fourth drop, he was cold, wet, and miserable. He hiked out of the river. It just wasn't worth continuing. A portage was the best option.

It may be tempting to sail over the waterfall with the organization, but don't do it. Listen for the signs of trouble and get out while you can. You may wander around on the shore for a while, but at least you will have the opportunity to plunge back in later. You will live to paddle another day. This is a crucial survival skill. Is your organization dealing effectively with the turbulence in your environment? Are people worn out and battered? Do you hear the roar of a waterfall ahead? Is there a place that you can see to pull out of the water and portage around this waterfall? Know how to recognize a bad situation and get out. Think *Titanic*. Think Eskimo.

> **The equivalent of a waterfall in an organization is a situation that threatens your sanity, your physical health, or your safety. Going on could mean emotional or even physical death.**

STRATEGIES FOR SCOUTING
AND PORTAGING

To navigate this turbulent environment, you can't depend on looking up to the control room. You need to look out to the water and make sense of what is going on. You need to spot the hidden obstacles and find the clear passages. You must look for places where you need to portage and get out while you can. Others can offer some insight into what lies ahead and where to go, but you need to find your own way.

Listen to the River: Read the Water

Scout. Listen to the world around you. Take the time to look downstream. Employ any of various disciplines to help you see and then organize what you see. In short, develop the skill of pattern recognition. Build the capacity to construct an accurate picture from bits of data.

In a world of rapid change, individuals need to learn to read the river and recognize the warning signs for themselves. On stretches without specific dangers or clear passages, one trip leader would shout to the other kayakers in the group to "R&R, baby." He wasn't talking about "rest and relaxation." He was telling them to "read and react." Read the water as you go through the rapid and react to what you see. The river you experience might differ markedly from the one found by the person immediately in your wake. You have to understand where you are and make sense of it, find the clear passages, and identify the obstacles—on your own. Your guides can only give you general directions. You must read the water and pick your way on a specific course through the rapids on-the-fly. You don't have the luxury of doing five-year plans (and sometimes not even business plans).

Sometimes the river will literally change overnight. Rob's friend Lori recalls coming up to the last rapid on the Tohickon Creek in Pennsylvania one day when they saw something unusual. The rapid at Pyramid Rock usually presents little challenge. This day it presented a line across the breadth of the river—the kind of feature that you typically don't see in nature. They pulled out and scouted. It turned out that a tree had fallen across the creek, creating an impassible "strainer," which poses a serious risk for pinning a kayaker. They wisely portaged. The paddlers who had made runs earlier in the day had said nothing about it—because it wasn't there. The tree had not yet fallen. The group that came down the river in the afternoon couldn't rely on old maps, their past experiences, or even the experiences of those who came down this same stretch of water earlier. They had to read the water on their own, in the moment, and react to it.

You might just have time to climb the bluffs above a rapid and pick out a route through the rocks and waves—and sometimes you might not have that luxury. At any level in the organization, you need to make a quick assessment of your resources and threats, and then move quickly to capitalize on the opportunities. You need to read and react.

What are you looking for? Primarily you look for threats and clear passages. The threats might come from massive holes or dangerous rocks, the clear passages flows of water where you can pass relatively unmolested. In business, companies engage in SWOT analysis—looking at their own Strengths and Weaknesses and the Opportunities and Threats in their environment. Individuals now need to do a similar analysis of their own environment. How could the subprime mortgage crisis or recalls of toys in China affect your own work? Could you outsource your personal assistant? What does the rise of MySpace and YouTube mean for your future customers and marketing? Data flows all around us, but we often don't take the time to think about what it means, to convert it to information. In looking at this data and your own work, pay attention to your own intuition. Interpret the shifting patterns for yourself. Is there something that doesn't feel quite right? If so, look a little closer.

What opportunities and threats exist around you in your work or in your industry? How will they affect your future? Do you have the right strengths to meet them? How do your weaknesses make you vulnerable? The threats and opportunities may come from the broader environment, such as economic growth or decline, or they might come from within the organization such as a rival gunning for your job. You need to develop the habit of reading your own environment, of not waiting for someone at the top of the organization to tell you what's what.

What strengths, weaknesses, opportunities, and threats reside in the moment? Make sure that you see some of each, because all exist all of the time in some form. What are the forecasts? A thunderstorm upstream can change the river in an hour or so. What did you see yesterday that might affect today or how might today foreshadow tomorrow? Keep a clear eye and an attentive mind.

Work through scenarios and plan alternate routes. If not A, then B, and if not B, then C. Far better to plan contingencies before an encounter with a demanding stretch of river. One's best thinking seldom occurs while pinned upside down under water, enhanced blood flow to the brain notwithstanding. Where in this part of the run might the trouble lie? How will you know? What are the three best alternate routes through these Class V rapids? Where is the one place you don't want to be? Where might you find a resting point, a temporary safe harbor?

Formulate hypotheses about what you think will happen and test them. Reconsider them in light of what unfolds. You want to know whether you had it right and why. The skill of debriefing, or what the military terms an "after action review," lies at the center of skill improvement and self-development. It is not a euphemism for negative feedback, because it encompasses, or should, both positive shaping data ("do more of that") and negative shaping feedback ("best to stop doing that").

> Your guides can only give you general directions, so you must read the water and, in the moment, pick your way down river through the rapids.

Develop Your Intuition and Then Listen to It

On June 3, 1805, Lewis and Clark faced a dilemma. They had followed Jefferson's instructions to explore the Missouri River. They had sought out counsel from local Native Americans, listened closely, and heeded their advice. No one, occidental or Native American, had mentioned the intersection of two major rivers they now studied. Which one should they follow? Or, as Lewis wrote in his journal, "An interesting question was now to be determined; which of these rivers was the Missouri?"

Interesting indeed. Time was of the essence, and a mistake could prove extremely costly. "To mistake the stream at this period of the season, two months of the traveling season now elapsed, and to ascend such stream to the rocky mountain or perhaps much further before we could inform ourselves whether it did approach the Columbia [River] or not, and then be obliged to return and take the other stream would not only lose us the whole season but would probably so dishearten the party that it might defeat the expedition altogether." They were at a turning point. Make the right choice at this unexpected point of choice or risk the entire expedition. Most of the United States' claims to what would become the Rocky Mountain and West Coast states hung upon this decision.

The North looked most like a continuation of the Missouri—same color water, same flow. Indeed, Lewis wrote, "the air & character of this river is so precisely that of the Missouri below that the party with very few exceptions have already pronounced the N. fork to be the Missouri." The "exceptions" were only Lewis and Clark themselves. The two of them believed that the change in the color and clarity of the water heading south fit with Native American descriptions of the Missouri River as coming from the mountains.

Lewis and Clark did not have much time. Still, they took valuable days to collect more data, to scout. Lewis took a small party north and Lewis took a small party south. Arduous, demanding, rain-soaked investigation led Lewis and Clark to hold to the choice of taking the south fork. The clarity of the water from the south fork seemed to fit the Native American descriptions of a mountain fed river. And the north fork simply went too directly north—that is, in the wrong direction.

Lewis and Clark presented these arguments to their men, but the men were unimpressed. They believed the north fork was the right choice. The dissenters included Cruzatte, an experienced waterman and "old Missouri navigator" who "had acquired the confidence of every individual of the party." Throughout their journey, Lewis and Clark listened closely to their men, to their guide Sacagawea, and to the Native Americans they encountered. They would hold votes, including one after they reached the Pacific about where to camp for the winter, a vote of historic symbolism for it involved a full vote for Sacagawea (a Native American and a woman) and York, Clark's African-American slave. Still, it was not a democracy. And here the two leaders of the Corps of Discovery felt they needed to trust their own intuition.

Lewis and Clark chose the south fork. Their men so respected Lewis and Clark's leadership that they followed without grumbling even though they thought it was the wrong decision. "They said very cheerfully that they were ready to follow us any where we thought proper to direct but that they still thought that the other was the river." The evening included a celebration and even music from the so recently over-ridden river expert Cruzatte.

It turned out that Lewis and Clark were right, their intuition spot on. That was the good news. The bad news was that one of the sure signs of the correctness of their intuition came with their arrival at the Great Falls two weeks later, as discussed later in the chapter. Yes, they had undeniably chosen correctly, *and* the course would prove more difficult than they had imagined. Intuition got them there—and a lot of sweat and toil took them around the falls to the Pacific.

Pay attention when your "spidey sense" tingles. Sometimes the passages are not at all clear. There may be times along the way when we stand like Gandalf in the caves of Moria in J.R.R. Tolkien's *The Lord of the Rings*. He and his companions lost deep in the earth, Gandalf, the group's leader, sniffs the air and ultimately chooses the way that *smells less foul*.

Often, we refer to this capacity to sense what is going on as "intuition." Books such as *Blink* and *Deep Smarts* have highlighted the advantages of pattern recognition, including speed and accuracy. Understand the power of intuition as well as techniques that help to develop this crucial whitewater skill, techniques such as guided practice, guided observation, guided problem solving, and guided experimentation. Intuition is not the same as hunches or dumb luck. When it works, it rests on deep understanding and experience.

Like a policeman who comments that the neighborhood does not feel right or a captain on deck who says the ship feels in order, one can come to know before knowing why one knows. The policeman can, on request, pause and then enumerate the cues that indicate something amiss. The captain can report the feel of the deck harmonics and the choreography of his crew's movements. An experienced paddler has reflexes and senses that help in finding passages or responding to unexpected threats.

Intuition can not only help you spot danger but also alert you to opportunity. In 1969, an inventor brought a new volleyball game for review by an elderly senior executive at Parker Brothers. This gray-haired man was a legend in the toy industry. The inventor and his team prattled on about the indoor volleyball game they had devised using a four-inch foam ball. To their irritation, the executive played, apparently distractedly, with the game ball as they walked through graphs and charts. Was he paying any attention? Had he finally "lost it?"

Suddenly he spoke, "Forget the game; keep the ball." The ball was the Nerf ball. It was introduced by Parker Brothers as the first "official indoor ball." By the end of the first year, they had sold more than four million balls. Soon a host of Nerf products grew out of this success.[4] The executive could pick out the important amidst the flotsam. He had the skill to recognize patterns, to take a point or two of data and derive meaning accurately.

You can develop the ability to read the water by spending time with an experienced paddler. In medicine, surgeons learn by the principle of "see one, do one, teach one." Watching and doing is guided practice. Watching itself benefits from "borrowing the eyes of another." The river presents far more to the trained eye than to the untrained. Socrates asked and asked in order to guide inquiry, so too does the whitewater journeyer benefit from guided inquiry to learn problem solving, to put technique to work on the river.

> ## Pay attention when your "spidey sense" tingles. Intuition can not only help spot danger but also alert you to opportunity.

 READING THE WATER

A downstream V can often signal a clear passage while an upstream V can signal the presence of a submerged obstacle such as a rock. A horizon line is often the sign of a significant drop, although it might be anything from an easy rapid to a deadly waterfall. In addition to finding clear passages, kayakers need to look out for rocks, "keepers," and eddies as they make their way down the river. Paddlers also need to be on the lookout for hazards such as undercut rocks or "strainers," trees that have fallen across the river. Experienced travelers on a given river can offer insight on the best routes. So, ask. Listen attentively and respectfully. Ultimately, of course, it comes down to you in the moment reading the water right in front of you, but others can help you to prepare for that moment.

In organizations, individuals cannot expect corporate leaders to tell them exactly where they are going. What you do in your job can differ significantly from your official (and outdated) job description. Sometimes you may need to "lead up," identifying potential hazards or new routes for the group or its formal leader. You need to be sure of where you are, to be sure of where you are headed and why. What is the world trying to tell you? Don't expect that someone will serve up an understanding of your work and your environment in a PowerPoint presentation in a conference room. You have to create your own view of the world and find your own path.

Listen to Others: Learn from Reports of Fellow Travelers

Lewis and Clark sought information from everyone they met, and many of the Native Americans who had explored the West provided insight on the journey ahead. These insights hardly qualified as precise Triptiks or detailed guides ("at mile 1,428, there will be a 90-foot rushing waterfall," and "watch for the grizzly at mile 745"). The information was general—about large waterfalls or mountain ranges—but helped to frame Lewis and Clark's own observations.

Listen to your fellow travelers. Learn to listen well. Study the process of active listening. Ask clarifying questions. Understand their stories. Attend to the entire message—spoken and unspoken, verbal and nonverbal, cognitive and emotional. You will learn much—about what lies out there, who they are, and, probably, who you are. All of that could come in handy at some point downstream.[5]

On an ocean liner, you focus primarily within the organization. You look to the officers for direction; you focus on your work at hand. You might not even attend to the larger world unless it intrudes on your particular piece of work. In permanent whitewater, however, you must focus on the world surrounding the immediate task, group, or even organization. You have to see the environment through which you travel. You have to adjust your course and make your own decisions about where to head and how best to arrive at whatever destination you have chosen. If you concentrate on life within your organization, you may well recognize significant changes in the water surrounding your vessel far too slowly.

Furthermore, do not get trapped in the iconic, sound-bite thin gruel that we receive daily. To do so risks simplifying, too often deceptively and even dangerously so, our reality. Remember the quote, "If everyone is thinking the same way, then someone isn't thinking." Then remember who said it—that icon of unrelenting, bulldog individual will: General George S. Patton. Years ago, Greg spoke to a former member of George S. Patton's HQ staff, a man who was now finishing a managerial career. About 50 years earlier, he had lied about his age and joined the American WWII army as an underage volunteer. He ended up serving with Patton. This staffer spoke of how he did not recognize the icon of Patton as the leader he served. There was truth to the public image, but in day-to-day interactions Patton attended to and sought the opinions of his staff. The man described Patton as the best boss he had ever had.

Remember the distinction between a good and a great conversationalist. A good conversationalist leaves you thinking how interesting and stimulating *they* are. A great conversationalist leaves you thinking how interesting and stimulating *you* are. People all have a story. They all know part of the river. Whitewater can be lonely and overwhelming. Knowing that you share the trip helps all travelers in times of trouble. Their experience also can help you better understand what lies ahead.

Two current practices warrant note here. Neither sweeps the landscape, but both have grown in popularity, and both testify at least to the felt need to receive the informed counsel of others. First, use life coaches. They are not psychologists or therapists, but are more like "personal trainers."[6] They do not require credentialing (although this has generated some controversy), and yet perhaps 10,000 life coaches practice in the United States. The growth and prominence of this service testifies to people's need to sort themselves out amidst the swirl of whitewater that surrounds them.

Second, use life boards or roughly what Kathy Kram and Belle Ragins term "developmental networks." A life board amounts to a personal board of directors but with only advisory and not governing powers. A person requests that people, usually already known and trusted, join his or her life board. Then, perhaps once or twice a year they meet, usually not as a board but rather one-on-one. At the meeting, board members consider current challenges and opportunities, ideally with a personal perspective and a long-standing perspective on the person. Recompense comes in the form of reciprocal service, continued contact, network building, or a good meal. Several of Greg's clients have established life boards, some explicitly, some implicitly. Again, the overriding point here comes down to the felt need to connect with others to gain perspective on one's self and on the river.

> Listen to your fellow travelers. Learn to listen well. You will learn a lot—about what lies out there, who they are, and, probably, who you are. All that could come in handy at some point downstream.

Know When to Portage

When Lewis and Clark reached the Great Falls on the Missouri, the sight was breathtaking. Meriwether Lewis called it the "grandest sight I ever beheld" with foam flying up 15 or 20 feet, and an arching rainbow across the roaring falls. These falls were nearly 90 feet high and 900 feet across. They welcomed the sight, at first, because it showed them they were on the right course. Then came the portage, one of the most exhausting and difficult phases of their entire 8,000-mile journey.

The winter before, they were told by their Native American hosts that the portage around the Great Falls would be about a mile and take about half a day. Nonetheless, in scouting the portage, Lewis and Clark found four more waterfalls. They and their company would have to hike more than 18 miles up the bluffs and back to the river to get around the five falls. It would take almost a month. They left their heaviest boat and equipment at the base of the falls and cut down cottonwood trees to make two crude carts. Using these carts, they dragged and pushed their remaining gear and six dugouts, each weighing about 1,000 pounds empty, along the perilous portage.

The ground was rocky, the sun harsh. Hail and rain pummeled them. The needles of prickly pear cactuses stabbed them, shredding the leather of their moccasins, which they had to replace every few days. Gnats and mosquitoes pestered them. Rattlers and grizzlies threatened them. Clark wrote that "To state the fatigues of this party would take up more of the journal than other notes which I find scarcely time to set down." When they reached the end of the portage, they had to build new boats to continue on their journey west.[7]

It took them almost a month of backbreaking labor to cover nine miles of river. In contrast, they had covered more than that distance going upstream on the river *in a single day* in the weeks preceding their arrival at the falls.[8] But when you face a 90-foot waterfall, staying on the water is not an option. At such points along the river, you have no choice but to portage. Like Lewis and Clark, you have to recognize this and do the difficult work to get around this obstacle.

How do you know when what you face could kill? On the river, the roar of the waterfall, spray shooting in the air, and a rainbow arching over the top signals that something is seriously amiss. You just don't see that on a normal day on the river. Pay attention and look for a place to pull out before the current becomes too swift.

In an organization, one of the signs of a waterfall is burnout. A classic study of burnout was conducted by Christina Maslach and Susan Jackson.[9] In their studies of the professional staff of human services institutions, they developed the Maslach Burnout Inventory (MBI), focusing on three primary dimensions:

- *Emotional exhaustion:* Feeling emotionally drained by one's contact with other people
- *Depersonalization:* Negative feelings and cynical attitudes toward the recipients of one's service or care
- *Reduced personal accomplishment:* A tendency to evaluate negatively one's own work

Do you recognize any or all of these signs? If you do, you are headed over the waterfall. Get out of the water. Take a vacation or leave your job. Use the pacing skills discussed in Chapter 2, if you can. But perhaps you can't. Your organization might effectively prohibit vacation or even adequate sleep. The demands might grow steeper and steeper. The backflow might become grabbier. Get help if you can; then find a way to live that will keep you alive. This type of situation could endanger your career or your health. Researchers have found that burnout was associated with job turnover, absenteeism, and low morale. It also appeared to contribute to personal distress, physical exhaustion, insomnia, increased use of alcohol and drugs, and marital and family problems. In short, it can lead to a steep and deadly descent.

Richard Boyatzis and Annie McKee write extensively about how leaders who are burnt-out first lose empathy and compassion before they become irritable and irritating.[10] They become dissonant and they infect others. They become less effective as leaders, even counterproductive. At this point, they may do more harm than good to themselves and to others by staying in the water.

Another sign that you have met a waterfall in organizational life might be as simple as a performance review. Poor job performance can indicate a need to change your habits or approach, or develop new skills. Maybe you need to accept the negative feedback and act on it. Or perhaps you are poorly matched in skills or temperament to the job at hand. Or maybe the problem lies in a profound lack of appreciation for your valuable contributions. To continue to do something that you cannot succeed at it is a sure-fire way to drown. Lacking a way to improve matters, get out of the water.

You might need to portage because you have an abusive boss or are in an untenable work situation. In the movie *Swimming with Sharks*, Kevin Spacey plays the studio baron Buddy Ackerman, the boss from hell. The boss mercilessly terrorizes and abuses his assistant Guy (Frank Whaley). Ackerman calls Guy names, throws coffee at him, and harasses him at home at all hours of the night. The assistant ultimately reaches the end of his rope and takes Ackerman hostage. Guy ties his boss to a chair, threatens him with a gun, and tortures him as payback. In a telling scene in the film, as he is tied to a chair and being beaten and abused, Ackerman points out to the assistant that he could have left anytime he wanted. Guy didn't want to give up this position in the office of his powerful boss. The assistant was so enmeshed that he didn't even realize the option of portaging. Perhaps the assistant had gone over the line crossed by many abused people, believing that he merited the abuse. If you have the boss from hell (or even Purgatory), ask yourself: Why are you staying there? Shouldn't you portage while you still have the strength and sanity to do so?

> If you are headed over the waterfall, get out of the water. Take a vacation or leave your job.

Recognize When You Are Drowning

Other factors can prevent us from seeing the waterfalls ahead. Organizations might expect superhuman effort. Voices of others drown out the sound of the falls. People repeatedly point to an individual or group and say, "I just don't know how they do it!" or "They're miracle workers!" or "Every day they're in here first and out last; the place couldn't operate without them!" If you hear these words, particularly about yourself, beware. Recognize them as the roar of the falls.

Unless you happen to have a big red "S" emblazoned on your chest, this crazy pace will drive you crazy or wear you down and out. The organization has come to depend on superhuman effort to compensate for its under-designed, under-staffed, and/or just generally under-resourced operations. Heroism, and the stress that goes with it, becomes an expected part of organizational life. Those who fall into this vortex receive accolades that become addictive, but the system and its heroes live a co-enabled world until the hero wears out. The occasional heroic act from various team members shows commitment and resourcefulness. The regular, required heroic act from the same few people indicates a problem and suggests a looming personal tragedy.

This is a recipe for disaster, partly because the condition may be difficult to spot, having become "normal." Nonetheless, stress kills. Do you see yourself as a salmon bravely swimming upstream? You might want a new role model. The salmon is "the icon of persistence, self-sacrifice, even heroism. But the truth is more prosaic: Their own stress hormones kill the salmon. The stress hormones give them the enormous burst of energy needed for the trek but ultimately reach toxic levels."[11]

Then there's the more common consequence of heroism, simple exhaustion, as discussed in Chapter 2. Research has shown that people with a performance deficit due to lack of sleep are not aware of the deficit.[12] Observers might see them nodding off and researchers can detect lapses, but the exhausted person may paddle on unaware that they are about to doze off until they actually fall asleep. Too often, employees will keep saying "yes" until they are overwhelmed and then it becomes impossible to think straight enough to say "no."

One reason that Robert E. Lee lost the battle of Gettysburg during the Civil War was because legendary cavalry leader Jeb Stuart wasn't there. At first, Stuart simply did not show up. Then, when he did appear, he appeared with an exhausted command. Stuart was there physically for the third and concluding day of the battle, but his worn out state and that of his troops contributed mightily to an uncharacteristic and ill-timed substandard execution of his duties. Stuart and his men rejoined Lee late because Stuart chose to conduct a long and grueling raid on his way north. By the time he reached Gettysburg, he, his men, and his horses were exhausted. He had expended their energy as if calm water lay ahead when, in fact and as he knew, a great and telling battle, a waterfall and a potential watershed, lay directly before them.

The stories astound. One of Stuart's men fell asleep on a split rail fence while climbing over. Another slept by an artillery battery as it exchanged fire with the enemy. Stuart himself apparently headed off in the wrong direction at one point, to be "turned around" by his staff. No time now to portage. A battle for a nation entered a third day, and Stuart had a part to play, but not the one he or Lee intended.

A grueling cavalry engagement east of the main battlefield may well have sealed the fate of Pickett's thousands of courageous infantry charging across open ground toward Cemetery Ridge. The engagement wore on. Stuart finally massed his horsemen and led a seemingly overwhelming force onto the field in an attempt to punch through stubborn Union resistance. Tired as they were, thousands of them neared their objective. Then, George Armstrong Custer led a charge of about 400 men against Stuart and his horde. That charge and the events it precipitated frustrated Stuart's mission of reaching the Union rear. This encounter may have decided the entire battle at Gettysburg. Stuart and his men had too little left when they were needed most.[13] They, Pickett, and arguably the Rebel cause sailed over the falls. Did they do anyone a favor by not honoring their physical limits and the nature of the river? Are you? Be aware of the warning signs (see following sidebar).

 SIGNS THAT YOU ARE HEADED FOR A FALL

Recognize when you are drowning. Boyatzis and McKee describe the biochemistry as well as the behavioral and effectual warning signs. Among these signs, ask yourself, am I:

- Working harder with less result
- Getting home later or leaving home earlier each day
- Feeling tired, even after sleeping
- Having trouble falling asleep, or waking up in the middle of the night
- Finding less time (or no time at all) for the things that used to be enjoyable
- Only really relaxed with alcohol

Have I noticed changes in myself or my relationships, such as:

- I can no longer really talk about my problems with my spouse.
- I don't care what I eat, or whether I eat too much or too little.
- I can't remember the last time I had a long conversation with a trusted friend or family member.
- My children have stopped asking me to attend their functions or games.
- I no longer attend my place of worship or find time for quiet contemplation.
- I don't exercise as much as I used to.
- I don't smile or laugh as much as I used to.

Ask yourself, do I:

- Have frequent headaches, backaches, or pain
- Routinely take over-the-counter antacids or painkillers
- Feel as if nothing I do seems to matter anymore, or have the impact I want
- Feel as if no one can understand what I need to do, or how much work I have
- Sometimes feel numb or react to situations with inappropriately strong emotions
- Feel too overwhelmed to seek new experiences, ideas, or ways of doing things
- Frequently think about how to "escape" my current situation

Be aware of when you are exhausted and act on this information. If you fall asleep crossing a fence or driving on the highway, see it as a sign of danger, a sign well worth heeding. Remember that if Jeb Stuart had understood the importance of arriving on time and in a reasonably rested condition, Gettysburg and possibly American history could have turned out differently.

> Do you see yourself as a salmon
> bravely swimming upstream?
> You might want a new role model.
> A salmon's own stress
> hormones kill it.

Listen to Your Heart

The shifts in relationships with a boss or the reasons for a portage can come abruptly, almost overnight, or they can develop over time. After more than a decade in a secure job in the Big Apple, Margeaux's life was filling out nicely. She had stayed with the same organization and risen to one level below the c-suite while still in her early thirties. She'd married recently and looked forward to starting a family. Only one major shadow crossed her life: her boss.

To her mind, he embodied a unique combination of incompetence and laziness. She had grown tired of both and their consequence, namely the need for her, as she said, to "carry his water." She decided on a potentially rash course of action: She went to talk to her boss's boss, the CEO.

He probably intended to provide support. He told Margeaux that he and the rest of the executive team greatly appreciated her work. He went on to say that they all knew the considerable limits of her boss, hence they were delighted that she had so ably taken over the actual running of her boss's function. In other words, they were not planning to make any change. So Margeaux made a change. A month later she quit. Time to portage.

She negotiated a substantial consulting contract with this organization and landed an additional one with another organization. Adequate cash flow secured, she and her still new husband went on tour. For months, they traveled the United States, visited friends, and looked for a place to land, a place with a good economy, a large airport, and exceptional skiing. They ended up in the West.

A year of consulting led to the discovery that Margeaux missed belonging to a real organization. Her network came to her aid, and she landed a job locally, no move necessary. The job amounted to a large step down in rank, and then there was the pregnancy. Margeaux told the CEO that she was in her first trimester. The CEO responded, "deliver a good six months analyzing that function and anything else I get will be a bonus." She could work with this boss. Margeaux signed on for the expedition.

Five years passed. Promotion followed promotion. Margeaux ended up at corporate. She discovered that she missed being closer to the action and moved back to the field. A second child arrived as did a new CEO. As the older child approached school age, Margeaux and her husband decided that, as much fun as this had been, this was not the place to raise or to school a child. This time personal decisions led them to portage. They began to look to the coasts.

A premier organization offered her a c-suite role. She visited the community and decided that it would not provide what she felt her family, especially her children, needed. She declined the offer. She trusted her heart.

Her network led another premier organization, if anything even more esteemed than the last, to offer her a seat in the c-suite. The offer, institutional reputation, better environs, and family ties led her to take the job. Several years and a promotion (or two) later made the decision look good. Margeaux plans to stay awhile. The moral of her story? In her words: "no matter where you go, there you are? Just kidding" More seriously, she added, "To paraphrase Max Depree 'You have to be willing to give up who you are to realize who you can become. Letting go of the known is the leap of faith that makes all the difference.'" You need to be true to yourself. Read the water. Listen to your own intuition. Chart your own course. Know when you need to get out and join something new. Your real job, in work, let alone life, is change.

When in Doubt, Scout

Sometimes you just can't tell what lies directly in front of you. Lewis and Clark experienced it. So, most likely, will you. The river might look like it drops off. It could be a bend in the river or a waterfall. The roar could be from rapids or a cascade racing into oblivion. Time to scout the rapids. It will take a little longer, but it will help you identify the traps and troubles ahead. This is what Lewis and Clark did when the reached the fork in the Missouri. They had little time, but they knew they needed to gather more information.

We have discussed how to scout and portage, but there is no set rule for *when* to scout or portage. You need to assess your own level of experience, comfort with the river, what you know about it, and what you are seeing and hearing as you approach a rapid. When in doubt, scout it. Attend to the river and your surroundings as you go. Don't wait for a crisis. You have nothing to lose by scouting, by focusing more on attending to your surroundings than on doing, save a little time and energy. If you fly blissfully and ignorantly downstream, then you could risk it all.

In your work, if you feel something is not right, take a closer look. Gather more information. Talk to others. If you feel worn down, then talk to trusted friends or family about your feelings. See if you can get a better read on what is happening. Is it a personal problem or is there something wrong with the organization? Is it mental or physical? Is it temporary or is it a permanent, possibly fatal problem? If you are not sure, or don't feel certain, spend the time to look a little more deeply. Get those medical tests. Get those psychological tests. Conduct your own reconnaissance. Figure out whether that roaring in your ears is coming from an undiagnosed auditory problem, an oncoming train, or a raging waterfall just ahead.

> **In your work, if you feel something is not right, take a closer look. Gather more information. Talk to others. See if you can get a better read on what is happening.**

THE PHOENIX

Whether you are going over the falls or the house is on fire, you should have one undiluted instinct: Get out. Don't sort through your valuables. Don't cling to the past. Don't ponder the meaning of life. Put your paddle in the water and head to shore. Race down the fire escape. Don't convince yourself that you can survive. Don't be phony tough or crazy brave. Grab yourself and your loved ones and get out into the air. Survival first.

Human beings have a remarkable capacity for healing and renewal. Even people on the brink of death can come back. A soccer team that crashed in the Andes; climbers after a disastrous ascent of Everest into "thin air;" Powell's crew who defied death on the Grand Canyon; Lewis and Clark and their Corps of Discovery who survived a perilous journey into the unknown—all these survivors lived to tell their tales because they managed to keep themselves alive. They knew to portage. Death is not reversible. You can recover from almost anything else.

The story of the mythical bird the phoenix embodies our wish for and testifies to our commitment to renewal. The phoenix builds a pyre every few hundred or a thousand years. Then it lights its nest on fire, completely destroying its old life in the process—or so it might seem. But from the ashes, there comes a stirring. And then a new phoenix flies out in all its glory. In dangerous, turbulent environments, this rising is part of the process. You will find yourself paddling through "the valley of death." Getting out of the river might end your old life. But fear not. Sure, rebuilding your life will be difficult, but don't think about it now. Stand outside in the glow of the fire, watching your old life crumble, or stand on the banks of the river and watch it go by. Take a deep breath and appreciate that you still stand. You have survived. You still seek to thrive. Soon you will rebuild. Soon a new life will emerge from the ashes. The portage may prove arduous, but soon you will plunge back into the river.

THE TAKEOUT

You can't expect someone else to tell you where you are going or what lies ahead; you need to look downstream, to attend to the signs of danger, to search actively for clear passage through or around whatever challenges or outright dangers the river holds.

CHAPTER 7

Rising Above the Roar
Communicate Through Symbols

We have an unknown distance yet to run, an unknown river to explore. What falls there are, we know not; what rocks beset the channel, we know not; what walls rise over the river, we know not.

—*Journal of John Wesley Powell, August 13, 1869, on the first descent of the Colorado River through the Grand Canyon*[1]

In 1969, a future client of Greg's arrived in Vietnam as a newly commissioned ROTC second lieutenant in the engineering corps. This 23-year-old had spent most of the previous few days traveling from the States. He was afraid as he contemplated the challenges ahead of him. The war was not going well, and he came from an increasingly divided nation. He came because, seemingly long ago, as he said, "I was just looking for a way to pay for college." He knew he represented a dangerous change for more experienced men facing an already turbulent and dangerous environment: a newly minted, masters-educated officer, an ROTC officer no less.

He stepped onto the small airfield bright and early, exhausted from days of travel from the States. A corporal in a Jeep greeted him with, "The captain wants to see you," and they were off. The young lieutenant entered his captain's tent. No greeting awaited him, just a map and an assignment: "Clear that area of mines by sunset," said the captain, pointing to the map. The lieutenant saluted and responded, "Yes, sir." What else could he say? He turned to leave. Then the captain offered, "And, lieutenant, welcome to Vietnam."

The lieutenant knew that clearing mines qualified as one of the worst and most dangerous assignments. He also knew that he and his new command, which he had yet to meet, had received the assignment because of him. He was fresh and therefore most expendable. His men were at risk in the first instance because he was expendable and in the second instance because of his absolute and relative lack of field experience.

He headed off with great trepidation to meet his command, the men with whom he would work, live, and perhaps die. Exhausted and scared, he pondered how to introduce himself to them and to this assignment. He had considerable formal authority. He was their officer. What he lacked was expertise in the task at hand, and he had no relationship with these troops. Tossed into whitewater, he had to sink or swim.

The lieutenant assembled his command and introduced himself. "I'm your new platoon leader. I've received my first assignment from the captain. It's to clear a field of mines. Now, I know that this is a shitty assignment, and I know that he gave it to us because of me. That's why I say that I received this assignment: I'm new; I'm most expendable. Hence, I'll clear the field. It's not fair for you to be placed in danger because of me. However, if I do this all by myself I'll most likely kill myself within the first few minutes and you'll end up clearing the field yourself anyway. I'm asking if you'd come with me and teach me. Stand as far behind me as you want as I do this, but teach me how to do it."

So, as the lieutenant describes it, "I spent my first day as an officer in Vietnam in a muddy field, mostly on my hands and knees, finding, disarming, and removing land mines. My men stood a few meters behind me. They watched what I did and regularly called me back to them for instruction—'Lieutenant, don't do that!' or, 'Don't move, lieutenant. Now listen to me.' or 'Stop that, lieutenant. Stand up slowly. Retrace your steps to me.' I never had to do anything like that again, and we got on more than well enough from that day forward. That day, though, made the others possible. Otherwise, I would have paid the price every day."

He put his tail on the line, and thereby made the strongest of statements. He communicated through behavior in a clear, transcendent, and symbolic fashion. He didn't just say he would put himself on the line for his men; he did put himself on the line. No one in his command needed a Rosetta Stone to translate what the young lieutenant was communicating. It was universal, and it was local, idiosyncratically and painfully so. It had nothing to do with any policy manual, rule book, or script. It was about them and him, there and then. It lived in the froth of the moment and helped him to survive the rest of the journey.

> He put his tail on the line, and thereby made the strongest of statements. He communicated through behavior in a clear, transcendent, and symbolic fashion.

STRATEGIES FOR COMMUNICATING ABOVE THE ROAR

The noise of turbulent environments makes communication difficult. One of the first casualties in permanent whitewater is language. In a stable organization, if you ask any employee what "loyalty" means, the conversation does not take long. But in a rapidly changing organization, you might never reach agreement on what it means. Language derives 70 to 80 percent of its meaning from context. Permanent whitewater shreds context. Hence, meaning becomes far more person-specific and far more dependent on relations with local reality and local people. Building those relations, in turn, rests more than ever on behavior and clear symbolic actions.

Actions Speak Louder Than Words

People in turbulent organizations go through a lot, including living seemingly countless "initiatives du jour" that amount to little save dashed hopes. These pilgrims often lack sufficient common history to lend many words common or shared meaning. They've heard it before. They're from Missouri, and their mantra is "show me."

The new leader who comes into an organization and speaks about a policy of openness may wax eloquent enough to challenge the Bard himself, but the roar of the rapids will drown out what seems to veteran whitewater kayakers so much droning. On the other hand, consider the executive who on her first day calls in workmen to remove the large wooden door to her private conference room and takes down the walls separating her office from the larger work area, yet speaks not a word. She captures the attention of all. She has sent a clear and unequivocal message thanks to the transcendent, symbolic nature of such an action. She means to work more collegially with others, regardless of rank, and she values making herself accessible. Message sent. Message received. No words needed.

In permanent whitewater, actions speak far louder than words. Data overload, jargon aplenty, and little meaning leave the field of communication crowded and littered. Nonverbal messages, including actions, offer the possibility of clear, emphatic, and memorable communication. On the river, paddlers sometimes use a set of arm-waving signals to stop or proceed (see the following sidebar "Using Signals on the River"). Paddlers often carry whistles attached to their life jackets so they can be heard above the noise of the rushing water. Three short blasts are the sign of distress. Similarly, in business, focus on ways to cut through the din of the river.

> Language derives 70 to 80 percent of its meaning from context. Permanent whitewater shreds context. Communication rests more than ever on behavior and clear symbolic actions.

USING SIGNALS ON THE RIVER

Communication is difficult on a whitewater river, because of distance between paddlers and the roar of the rapids, so paddlers use a set of hand and paddle signals to communicate. Patting the top of the helmet with a hand both asks and answers in the affirmative the question, "Are you okay?" Anything but this response requires immediate action on the part of the other paddlers.

Swinging the paddle from side to side signals an emergency or a call to stop and gather up, while holding the paddle vertical is a sign that it is okay to go forward.

A paddle held horizontally calls for others to stop and hold their positions.

In turbulent organizational environments, rapid changes and differences in cultures make it difficult to communicate. In such environments, actions speak louder than words, and sometimes you need to make simple and dramatic statements to rise above the roar.

Maintain a Line of Sight

The need to communicate through nonverbal cues and actions also places special importance on maintaining a line of sight on the river. At the very least, you need to see the person ahead of you. The modern, turbulent business environment tempts us to fall back on virtual interactions. They take less time at that moment. They do not, however, provide the rich communication of face-to-face interactions. You need to maintain this line of sight more than ever.

If you cannot interact face-to-face all the time, at least engage in some face-to-face meetings up front. Such interaction supplies the human context for subsequent virtual interaction over the so-called broadband. Such interaction fosters greater understanding and yields greater sensitivity to even subtle cues. These cues might otherwise pass by team members unnoticed. Talk to all expedition members at the put-in before you enter the turbulence of the river. The group can establish ground rules and make general plans in this relatively calm space, a foundation that will be valuable once you enter the turbulence of the river. The details of any communication from a leader matter more than ever in the permanent whitewater environment.[2]

Meg Whitman, former CEO of eBay, understands. eBay qualifies as an icon of the Internet age, an organization that understands technology and moves at the speed of the Internet—except at her Monday staff meetings. When she was CEO, all Whitman's direct reports had to check their electronic devices at the door of the meeting room. They gathered to talk to each other, face-to-face, before moving at the speed of the Internet. She said, "Personal interaction is much more important than instantly answering e-mails." In other words, the leaders of one of the world's fastest moving organizations pull over to the side of the river at least once a week to slow down to the speed of face-to-face human interaction. That's the message. And the medium?—the symbolic and unmistakably clear action of checking one's electronic gear at the door.[3]

> The modern, turbulent business environment tempts us to fall back on virtual interactions. They take less time at that moment. They do not, however, provide the richness of communication of face-to-face interactions. You need to maintain this line of sight more than ever.

Never Risk a Lie—Even Unintentionally

Communicating in turbulent organizational environments involves a special risk, that of the unintentional lie. A manager may say to employees, "All you've got to do is get through this hour, this week, this month, and it will all go back to normal." This is a lie. The manager doesn't set out to lie, but at the end of the hour, the week, or the month, the report experiences the manager as having lied. In a steady state, change, steady state world, one can speak with more certainty. After all, managers in that world should know just where they are headed. In a permanent whitewater world, however, much uncertainty characterizes the future. Furthermore, no one has enough control to permit them to make definitive statements about the future. In a permanent whitewater world, reality changes too quickly to make steady-state promises.

Imagine that you set out to run a race. Your boss tells you to sprint; it's a 40-yard dash. Just as you strain to break the tape, your boss arrives again and says: "Sorry! You know what? It's a 100-yard dash." Just as you approach that finish line, the boss tells you it's a 400m, then an 800m, and then a 5k and then a 10k. And as you drag yourself toward the finish line of the 10k, your boss appears again with a clipboard and says, "Trust me. I'd have been the first to tell you it was a marathon if I had known that this was a marathon. Kick it in gear!"

We've all probably experienced this situation, either as the boss or the employee. So much for success. So much for trust and truth. Running a marathon as a sprint does not lead to victory. It leads to failing to finish. It usually leads to race officials sending out a little truck in the dark to you to pick you up off the side of the road and hook you up to an IV drip. Sprints and marathons require different training and strategies. You need to know which you are running before you set out. Figure that you are in a marathon, a whitewater marathon, and speak accordingly or risk developing a reputation for lying (see the following sidebar "Little Whitewater Lies").

LITTLE WHITEWATER LIES

Consider a few other exchanges between managers and employees. In each case, bosses act as if they work in a steady-state world. They do not. Hence, they revise "truth," break promises, and erode trust—even as trust becomes an ever more important ingredient as groups need to form fast, relate and rely on one another fast, and produce fast:

Today the boss says: "Just take on this two-week project that needs to be done. It's critical and will eat you up over this period, but then we'll get you back to a normal schedule."

One week later: "Who would have thought! I need you to tackle this three-week project that just came up that is even more important than the two-week project. So, I know you're tired, but pick up the pace on that two-weeker so you can get on this three-weeker."

Today the boss says: "We have a unique international opportunity for you in Mexico City in June, July, and August. Just tackle this problem for us and then we'll bring you home and get you settled back down."

At the end of August: "Who would have thought! As a result of your success, you're the only person in the organization with this type of international experience. We need you for an important assignment in Spitzbergen for the winter. Pack heavy clothes. You'll be holed up for a few months in the winter without sunlight. Then, you'll come home, thaw out, and get back to normal. Promise. Oh, by the way, how's the family?"

Or consider another similar scenario of communications around downsizing:

Today the boss says: "We have a budget crisis. Downsized. You know the drill. We cut jobs and so I need you to take on Carlos's job since he was downsized. Just take this on for a couple of months until we can sort this out and get back to normal staffing. Who knows, maybe we will even hire Carlos back."

A couple of months later: "Who would have thought! They took another 10 percent out of the budget! Carlos isn't coming back. Nobody is coming back. The good news, though, is that you are still here, and you have two jobs now: yours and Carlos's. Maybe if we'd known this we would have handled things differently. Anyway you have two jobs, and I don't have money to pay you anything more. Sorry. Would you like a new title?"

What would a more honest approach be? The manager might say: "I need you to take on Carlos's job. I don't know how long it will be. I understand that it isn't humanly possible to do the jobs of two people. Figure out what you can cut out of your job and his job to make it work." This recognizes the basic truth that employees have limits, that the river runs long and white, and that everyone needs to keep a roll in reserve. It also acknowledges the limits of the manager's omniscience and provides a basic sense of direction and guidance for navigating downstream. And the truth makes your complicated life a little less complicated. As Mark Twain said, "If you tell the truth you don't have to remember anything."

> In a permanent whitewater world, reality changes too quickly to make definitive statements and steady-state promises.

Ensure Two-Way Communication

Corporate leaders acting in a steady state, change, steady state world can pronounce meaning within their organizations. In a permanent whitewater world, the ingredients of meaning often come more fragmented and from more and varied sources. On the ocean liner, the orders flow down the line of command. The captain only needs to look up occasionally to make sure the vessel is not headed toward an iceberg. In permanent whitewater, 80 percent of the work of the unit leader lies outside the unit and only 20 percent inside. The strategy and direction are not determined as much by what goes on inside the boat—setting a straight course across open waters—rather strategy and direction stem from what goes on outside the boat. Every member of the organization and not just the leader needs to make sense of their respective environment (both inside and outside the organization) and to relay that information back to others so that they can make their way safely downstream. You need to be able to listen to others and communicate to others, no matter where you find yourself within the organization. A single voice could represent the only notice of an opportunity or warning of danger ahead.

The techniques? First, adopt the mindset that followers matter. In America, we live in a society that emphasizes the value of leadership and yet seldom even notes the importance of thoughtful, competent followers. We laud the exploits of astronauts while comfortably overlooking the tens of thousands of people around the planet who make possible the voyage proper.[4]

Second, ask questions. Start with the most junior person present. Seek positives as well as negatives from everyone. Practice active listening. If no one responds, then provide more confidential channels (such as notes or surveys). Pay attention to the content and the affect. Ask questions about both and ask as nonevaluatively as possible (for example, "Would you say more about this?" or "How did you handle your fear?" and not "How could you have made that mistake or felt that way?"). Concentrate. Focus your attention and your eyes. Listening is hard work, just ask Socrates. Think of the next question that you want to ask to assist both of you to plumb the story further. When in doubt, ask "Why?"

Recall that even in a hierarchical setting such as the military, officers of rank can create space for active discussion and dissent. "Bars Off" meetings entail a commander dropping his or her hat on a table and symbolically removing rank insignias. He might do so on his own initiative or upon request by a direct report. Others present drop their insignias of rank into the hat as well. Then they all discuss "offline" whatever needs discussing before reclaiming their ranks and reentering their respective roles. In highly developed commands, these conversations can prove remarkably frank and helpful in clarifying various views of the river ahead and just what needs doing as a result.

> You need to listen to others and communicate to others, no matter where you find yourself within the organization. A single voice could represent the only notice of an opportunity or warning of danger ahead.

Create Space to Grieve: Funerals, Irish Wakes, Slicing Nursing Stations, and Other Symbolic Events

Turbulence induces change, and change often entails letting go. Places and ways of working drop behind. You sometimes need to say good-bye to colleagues. However necessary these losses, they count as losses nonetheless. You need to discuss them and to grieve for them.

Americans have a remarkable capacity to move through the present toward the future with little or no attention afforded to history. Yet, a pause to acknowledge the past can free one up for the journey through the present toward the future. In one organization, a junior executive received instructions to go and shut down a branch. This branch had a long history in the firm and had produced some noteworthy and even publicly acclaimed work. Closing it and moving the work to headquarters made sense financially, but emotions would run high. Providing the option to transfer to corporate, although not far away, would for many amount to an invitation to live with the proverbial mother-in-law after divorcing one's spouse. Having someone from corporate come to help might very well only add to a mood of solemnity and a feeling of resentment.

The change agent arrived in the branch office and soon assembled all hands. He announced his mission and a timeline of a few months. He also announced formation of a cross-functional, cross-level project team with three objectives: 1) to close the office on time, on budget, 2) to accomplish the objective in accordance with firm values and practices, and 3) to arrange for suitable acknowledgment and celebration over the upcoming months to honor what had transpired in the office over the years as well as the people who had made it all possible. The third objective came as a surprise to those gathered, as did the budget set aside to accomplish it. Message delivered through symbol and deed: We have to go, but things happened here that warrant recounting and celebration before we move on. The junior executive accomplished his mission, including drawing a much larger than expected number of employees from the branch to corporate.

A nurse manager faced a similar challenge. A clinical unit of long-standing and unusually high camaraderie would close. The space, indeed the building itself, would vanish. The staff would scatter across the hospital. In the meantime, patients needed care. Additionally, the hospital could use the staff given the acute need for all clinicians, especially nurses. The white hot labor market argued for low expectations about retaining staff from a dismantled and scattered, high performing, high morale unit.

The nurse manager set about her work. She established a cross-level, cross-functional team to plan and implement the shutting down of the unit. They also planned a festive closing event. Months later, the last patient left the unit and the work of saying farewell began. People gathered—current workers, past workers, and even former patients. Mementos went on the walls—letters, pictures, relics, totems, and photos galore. The room filled with the past. The selected mood and genre fit the ethnicity of many of the unit's staff: an Irish wake…without the alcohol. People cried, laughed, complained, and praised.

All of that was planned. What was not planned was what the nurse manager did as the event started to wind down. A member of the facilities department showed up with a power saw and cut the nursing station—the symbolic and functional center of any clinical unit—into pieces as if it were a large birthday cake. She then invited one and all to take a piece home with them. Remarkably, many chose to take some piece of veneer or plastic or wood with them. Perhaps not remarkably, patient care never faltered, the unit closed as scheduled, and *only one* clinical staff member chose to stop working at the hospital.

A major pharmaceutical company shut down one of its offices after a merger. On Friday, employees packed up their offices into boxes for shipping to the new headquarters 30 miles down the road over the weekend. At the close of the day, the 180 members of the staff gathered in the meeting room of the building for a celebration based on the popular *Survivor* reality television show, complete with tiki torches. The gathering provided the community a humorous way to come together to say farewell to the old office and embrace the new. Then, they voted everyone off the island.

Enterprising leaders have used mock wakes, funerals, and bar mitzvahs to mark closings and transitions. The chosen symbol has depended on the particulars of mood, people, and ethnicity. They shared a desire, if not the exact form, to acknowledge that something worth noting and worth mourning happened here. The voyage stops to pay tribute to the people, time, effort, and accomplishment. Stopping the journey just so helps people to continue it. Permanent whitewater brings rapid change. With rapid change comes loss. Recognize the loss and celebrate the journey so that you can move on down the river to the next rapid.

> Enterprising leaders have used mock wakes, funerals, and bar mitzvahs to mark closings and transitions. They acknowledge that something worth noting and worth mourning happened here. Stopping the journey just so helps people to continue it.

Make Sense of What Happened: Share Stories Around the Fire

In turbulent environments, stories help make sense. The stories we create and tell one another shape our understanding. They help us learn. They inspire us to plunge back into the stream. The confusion of turbulence mangles meaning. Stories give meaning back to us who travel through an environment that often muddies understanding and muddles our capacity to make sense.

Expeditions have a long tradition of sharing stories around the campfire or in writings after the fact. We value sharing what happened today, to us, what has happened before, to us and to others, and what may happen tomorrow, further down the river. We sort out our experiences. We learn. We connect with our fellow travelers, even across time.

Storytelling involves experiencing the event anew, in the present tense. We can feel our connection to events even as others come to connect to the event through us. Most effective storytelling involves the personal presence of the storyteller, ideally in the story and certainly in the emotional fullness of a re-creation. Key descriptors draw us into the scene and into the midst of characters, themselves of growing interest. A moment filled with the most human of implications defines the story and may offer a unique insight into one's self. The moment evokes emotion and special identification with those who created the story. We connect to others, to their lives, and to ourselves. Many an old tale of organizational life drifts shattered in the permanent whitewater world of today. They may have once sustained us, but now their remnants simply float about us. We need relevant stories to replace them.

Organizational leaders (and followers) should create opportunities for telling tales around the fireside, storytelling at the end of a day of paddling, tools to help us understand the triumphs and learn the lessons from shooting the rapids. We need to celebrate our wins. There are no natural breaks in the action in permanent whitewater, hence we need to make time and space for this reflection in our own lives and in our organizations. It is important to tell these stories face to face whenever possible, especially in this virtual age. The more intimate the telling, the greater and fuller the appreciation of the drama and treasure resident in our journeys.

> **The stories we create and tell one another shape our understanding. They help us learn. They inspire us to plunge back into the stream.**

Use Myths to Create Meaning

Myths propel us forward. They make sense of what has happened and lend meaning to what will happen. The journeys of others merge with our own as does the meaning of their lives merge with the meaning of our own. So we create myth, often of a highly personal nature.

Some stories that grow to myths transcend our personal journeys. They become broader myths that give meaning to our own work. Why does one plunge into the cold, turbulent water of a whitewater river? Is it just for money or for glory or for the thrill? Stories of others who have gone before can drive people into the unknown and support them along the way. How many mountain climbers have the exploits of Sir Edmund Hillary aided? How many paddlers on the Grand Canyon have carried Powell's diaries in their river bags? Reading the stories of others encourages us to pick up our paddles, to continue the journey, to make it our own, and perhaps thereby to add to it and to pass it on.

Dreams are vital in making such journeys. Dreams precede plans. Years ago a CEO phoned Greg. The conversation went something like this:

"Hi, I got your name from [another CEO]. I'm looking to construct a plan for my firm, and I understand that you do that work in a different and effective way. Would you help me construct a plan for my business?"

Greg responded, "What's your dream?"

The CEO said, "I want a plan."

"What's your dream?"

"I want a plan!"

"What's your dream?"

"I WANT a plan!"

Greg broke the brief do-loop, "We could probably do this back and forth a few more times, but let's stop here. Anyone can do a plan. I can give you names of a number of people who will work with you to construct a perfectly good plan. Yet, if you want to rise each day and lead, lead with enthusiasm—lead yourself, lead others—then you need to begin with your own dream, something dear enough to you that you will take it into your belly, grow it, go through the agony of birthing it, nourish it, and endure the trepidation of watching it struggle to go beyond you in order to stand on its own. Dreams enthuse leaders and keep them going. Enthusiastic leaders do the same for their followers. True enthusiasm is not a cloak put on like a costume. It comes from within; it comes from your dreams."

The CEO clipped a response, "Thanks," and hung up.

Months later Greg answered the phone to discover that the same CEO had called back saying, "Do you have a minute?"

Greg controlled his more sarcastic inclinations and declared simply, "Sure."

The CEO then read an approximately 50-word description of the emotions that he wanted to feel when he walked into the lobby of his headquarters. The description was personal. He concluded and asked, "Is that a dream?"

Greg replied, "Sounds like a dream to me."

Silence hung for a moment.

The CEO then queried, "NOW can we do a plan?"

And indeed we did.

All of us work to create meaning. Philosophy, of course, represents a full-time commitment to the creation of such meaning as can religion. Who are we? Why are we here? What should we do? What does it matter? These are all the stuff of the deeper stories of myth and meaning.

Myth has gotten a bad name. "Oh, that's a myth" comes now as an easy, offhanded dismissal of the ill-, mis-, or uninformed. The word, though, deserves a better fate. Historically, over millennium, myths have comprised the center of meaning. Myths portray the universe, its many manifestations and forces, ourselves in our many facets, and the relation between the eternal or transcendent and us and the temporal. Myths provided a key way to teach what truly mattered across time. Myths were the way we centered ourselves. Myths were the vehicles that provided the way to calibrate a life. Myths provided a way to navigate.

Leaders, in particular, need to share the stories that matter to them, that guide them. The stories may or may not involve them. The stories may feature the leader, those they have followed, or those who follow them. These myths create a texture of meaning, a way to navigate even, indeed especially, in the absence of the leader. Myths do not distract from the work at hand; they support the work by imparting guidance and imbuing meaning. Myth making precedes plan making. Myth follows any plan execution. Myth fills a plan with personal meaning. Myth proposes an answer to "Why?"

> Why does one plunge into the cold, turbulent water of a whitewater river? Stories of others who have gone before can drive people into the unknown and support them along the way. How many mountain climbers have the exploits of Sir Edmund Hillary aided? How many paddlers on the Grand Canyon have carried Powell's diaries in their river bags?

Use Metaphors

In communications, metaphors can also help to explain and understand our environment. In this book we have used the metaphor of permanent whitewater to explore organizational turbulence. We need to find metaphors for making our environment real to others. If we live in a world of basic stability or a world of jarring change followed by extended periods of basic stability, then the permanent whitewater metaphor does not fit and has little use. We, mankind, have created this permanent whitewater world. It is new and stems from globalization, changes in financial markets, and auto-catalytic technological advances. It is a product of our own hand, distinct from most of the natural world. So this natural image of permanent whitewater comes to fit this brave new world of our creation.

One SBU head at a major energy company left a course that Greg taught on change with a clear metaphor in mind. He went home filled to the brim with thoughts of the mindset change represented by internalizing the metaphor of permanent whitewater. He talked about it. He used it. He even found a clip of whitewater rafting and played it continuously on the huge public screen in the lobby of his headquarters. He wanted the metaphor to communicate the reality and to serve as a reference for his organization. He wanted it to create meaning. It became a powerful image for helping to focus and guide their work by providing a constant criteria for evaluation: Does a current or proposed action help the organization to deal with its permanent whitewater world? Can it succeed in the world shown on this screen?

> We need metaphors to capture the essence of our new world, and make our environment real to others. This natural image of whitewater comes to fit this brave new world of our creation.

FINDING MEANING AND SHAPING A LEGACY

The owner of a midsized and very profitable organization worked tirelessly, year after year. Each day he told himself why: He had a child with a severe and fatal birth defect. She would most likely die in her twenties. Each day he went off to work with a mantra: "She shall not want." His business, his success, his mission statements, they had meaning to him, because they provided the means to care for his daughter. Such was his myth that gave meaning to his actions, that guided him down the river.

The roaring swirl of whitewater simultaneously demands flexibility and directionality, adaptability and purposefulness. Much of this book thus far has stressed flexibility and adaptability, but such attributes without purpose or direction can too easily leave one circling a vortex or pinned against a rock. You need your own myth as a guide. What matters most to you? If you left your job in 3 or 5 years, what would have made it all—the wear and tear, frustration, and lost nights—worthwhile? When you get up each morning and prepare to reenter the rapids, what do you say to yourself about why you are doing so? When you die, what do you want said about you? In short, what gives your effort meaning, to you? Lacking that answer amounts to lacking a compass. The froth and frenzy of the river engulf the aimless.

Navigating well has always presented challenges. Getting there and back demands navigation, and no one wants to be lost. In particular, no one wants a leader to be lost—lost leader, lost followers. Navigation at work, let alone in life overall, involves selecting one's own stars by which to steer. Choices today include which river, when, how far, how fast, and with whom.

Great and compassionate minds have come time and again to this question of meaning and life. In modern times, Viktor Frankl, describing the internal resources that allowed him to survive the Auschwitz concentration camp, states in *Man's Search for Meaning* that "once an individual's search for a meaning is successful, it not only renders him happy but also gives him the capability to cope with suffering."[5] Meaning comes down to "becoming aware of *what can be done* about a given situation."

And the route to meaning? Frankl says that there are three paths. First, create work or perform a deed. Second, truly experience someone else—that is, love. Third, rise above one's suffering—we all suffer pain in our lives, but what we do with the suffering, with our crucible, defines us. Starkly, "in the filth of Auschwitz…individual differences did not 'blur' but, on the contrary, people became different; people unmasked themselves, both the swine and the saints." There are few more confusing, turbulent, and horrifying environments than a concentration camp. And yet, Frankl and others were able to find meaning there. In fact, in a real sense their created meaning was what kept them alive.

Pounding whitewater notwithstanding, each of us defines the past, the present, and the future in the stream of our lives, and so, in part, we also define the river of time itself. We in the West especially live in a "do it yourself" world. Technology and material prosperity provide a wealth of options for how we spend our time let alone how we define ourselves. The range of approved, protected, or at least tolerated life values and lifestyles can stagger us. Our ancient European headwaters fed this combination of tools and choices even as our ever-increasing technology and individual freedom sped the river and led it to boil. Yet, the good news here, the overwhelming good news, is that these choices create more options than ever for us. In short, we choose which river to run, how to run it, and to what end—doing so makes all the difference in the moment and in the moments that follow.

The ancient Celts offered the following guidance for life: Do not do what you do because you expect some reward from the gods, for such is not their nature. Do not rage at the gods for not providing a reward, for such is the action of a child. Do what you do, choose what you choose, because it defines your life—indeed it defines life itself.

We do not get to decide when or where we die, but we do have the opportunity to determine for what our lives stand. Alfred Nobel, then best known as the inventor of dynamite, picked up a French newspaper in 1888 to read his own obituary. His brother Ludwig had died, and the newspaper published Alfred Nobel's obituary by mistake. It gave him a chance to see how he would be remembered. It was not a pretty picture.

The headline read: *Le marchand de la mort est mort.* ("The merchant of death is dead.") It said that he had built his fortune by enabling people to kill one another more efficiently.[6] Nobel had always seen himself as a pacifist and thought that the invention of dynamite and other explosives would bring an end to war. Two armies armed with such weapons would have the sense to put down their arms. (Like the creators of missiles called "Peacekeeper," he seriously overestimated the rationality of such combatants.) Reading his obituary, he seemed destined to be remembered as the inventor of one of the most destructive forces ever created. It was a sobering moment.

When Nobel actually died in Italy on December 10, 1896, he left 31 million Swedish kronor (more than $9 million) to establish a set of prizes in physics, chemistry, physiology or medicine, literature, and peace. His family was shocked to see their fortune lost. Swedish officials worried about such a large fortune leaving the country. But by 1901, the first Nobel Prizes were awarded. Today, we remember Nobel for this ongoing testimony to the best in ourselves. He had rewritten his legacy.

In a whitewater environment, your meaning and legacy may not come from the position you hold in a company. The position or the company may not exist tomorrow. You need to determine your own mythology, write your own story, and shape your own legacy. Like Alfred Nobel, you have the power to determine the meaning of your life.

In a whitewater environment, your meaning and legacy might not come from the position you hold in a company. The position or the company might not exist tomorrow. You determine your own mythology, write your own story, and shape your own legacy.

THE TAKEOUT

Whitewater shreds meaning, so you need to use actions, stories, and myths to make sense of the chaos and give meaning to the journey.

CHAPTER 8

Building Flocks
Teaming for Today's Run

Though this be madness, yet there is method in it.
—William Shakespeare

Tracy's position was secure. Not yet 40, she had spent more than a dozen years with an organization that grew steadily despite a difficult and turbulent environment. A high-potential junior executive, she enjoyed various assignments and participated in the inner circle of leaders just below the executive suite. A few more years and she would most likely enter the suite herself. She and her family had settled into a community for keeps. She did not plan to go anywhere else.

The world changed. New colleagues demonstrated a significantly different orientation to the business and, more important to her, to the people in their organization. The job was the same, but she no longer felt connected to the team. This cross-current unsettled her. Finally, one night, she said to her husband, "I'm thinking about leaving." From then on, something changed. She began to look for a way to get out of this river, leave this team, and join a new one. She scouted with a half-hearted job search. She received an offer to enter a new industry in a dramatically different type of firm—smaller, entrepreneurial. She took it. She would never look back.

As she drove to her first day of work, however, she received news that the entrepreneurial CEO had sold the firm. This river had turned more turbulent than she had expected. The owner, a key part of her decision to join the organization, became an employee and, predictably, soon left. The new owners were energetic, young, and not very skilled. Still, she tried hard to make this run down this new river work. She learned new skills. She prospered. But this was not for her. She wanted out.

A senior executive from her former organization asked to meet with her: What would it take to get her back? A domain of her own away from her former boss and colleagues, she said. Done. In about a year, she sat down with the CEO who asked her if she would like to join the senior executive team in a newly created role. Would she be interested in an expanded version of her former boss's job? She signed on. She had left this team, joined another, and then come back.

Throughout your career, you will make choices about the teams you join. In whitewater, these teams tend to be more fluid, more ad hoc. You need to know who you are, how you fit into the team, when to stay put, and when to find a new team. You need to stay true to yourself while being part of a group. This might mean a highly flexible approach to your career. As Tracy sums up her experiences, "Work hard. Do the right thing. Keep your eyes open. Don't be afraid."

> In whitewater, these teams tend to
> be more fluid, more ad hoc. You
> need to know who you are, how you
> fit into the team, when to stay put,
> and when to find a new team.
> You need to stay true to yourself
> while being part of a group.

MURMURATIONS OF STARLINGS: TEAMS HAVE A LIFE OF THEIR OWN

Every fall and winter vast flocks of starlings gather in Rome. These birds travel together in unison, weaving back and forth in huge coordinated clouds across the sky before settling on the train station and other buildings. Unlike geese in formation, they have no clear leader. Yet these starlings oscillate together as if they have one mind, as many as 50,000 at a time, in what is called a "murmuration." They go banking and vibrating back and forth in the evening sky as they return from foraging for olives in the countryside. Trained pilots would take years of practice to perfect these aerial maneuvers—if they could ever pull them off—yet these synchronized flights appear effortless to these natural Blue Angels.

The starlings in Rome have attracted a flock of two-legged human researchers who observe their movements. Studies of these birds there and in other parts of the world have indicated that the actions of the birds can be described by a simple set of rules:

alignment, separation, and cohesion. The birds move in the general direction of the birds in their vicinity, keep a certain separation from those around them, and demonstrate cohesion with their flock mates. While scientists initially thought the birds referenced others in a certain radius, researchers discovered that the birds actually reference a small group, maybe six or seven, in their immediate vicinity. This reference allows them greater flexibility or, restated, less constrained, faster decision-making.

Such swarming behavior in birds, fish, or bees looks intelligent and orchestrated. It manifests a certain intelligence of its own, yet it is not the result of command and control. Instead, it results from the initiative of thousands of independent actors whose movements add up to an impressive whole. All of this suggests an entirely different way of thinking about organizing, managing, and living within large groups.

In 1986, Craig Reynolds created a computer model to simulate the coordinated actions of birds in flocks or fish in schools. He called his virtual creatures "boids" and set them loose to soar back and forth across computer screens. The animation appears so lifelike that it became the basis for the cinematic movement of a flock of penguins running down the streets of Gotham City in Tim Burton's 1992 film *Batman Returns*. This behavior certainly differs from the more ordered outcomes of controlled systems, yet no one should confuse it with chaos. It exists in a space described as "the edge of chaos"[1] and represents the principle of emergence, where complex behavior in large groups emerges from simple local rules.

Kayakers depend on similarly ad hoc and loosely coupled teams. When navigating a rapid, a boater may only see a boat or two ahead or behind. Each boater keeps a line of sight with the others if possible. Yet the team finds its way through rapids, each boat following the one before it. There is separation and cohesion. Everyone is loosely aligned in moving downstream. Typically a boater with experience on the river goes ahead either to show the best line or to serve as a "canary in a coal mine" to identify the potential dangers. If this pioneer gets caught in a hole, then others know to avoid it.

> When navigating a rapid, a boater might only see a boat or two ahead or behind. Yet the team finds its way through rapids, each boat following the one before it. Everyone is loosely aligned in movement downstream.

STRATEGIES FOR TEAMING

Modern organizations qualify as flatter, more project-based, and more temporary. This permanent whitewater world mandates more ad hoc relationships. You will spend more of your career teaming, which means more attention to setting up and taking down teams, more fluid roles, and the need for better communication, negotiation, and coalition building. On an ocean liner, everyone has a clear role. If an engineer quits, the leader advertises for a new engineer and hires someone with a clearly defined set of skills. This person may have other skills and qualities such as courage that could come in handy when the iceberg hits, but these are not usually part of the job description. The clearly defined job enables a clear delineation of required skills and employees with this particular set of skills become as interchangeable as parts in a machine. Of course, this oversimplifies the ocean liner world, where extraordinary individuals can make a difference. Still, the primary way of organizing rests on fixed roles and clear jobs. Onboard the ocean liner, the organizational structure is fixed and clear. Every employee has a clear role in the chain of command that runs down from the captain at the helm to the sailors in the engine room.

A flock of starlings, however, is not a machine. As the clear roles in your organization break down, you need more fluid skills and structures. You need to adjust and adapt and find your own way while keeping track of those around you. In paddling, the group possesses a collective intelligence, but at the end of the day each person is in his or her own boat. In permanent whitewater, teams form and reform quickly, as needed and on an ad hoc basis. Briefly stated, teams adjust to their environment by how they form and reform into teams as well as in how they act as teams. Each paddler is an independent entity yet needs to function as part of a group, however temporary. As a starling moving in one of these murmurations, what should you do?

> As the clear roles in your organization break down, you need more fluid skills and structures. You need to adjust and adapt and find your own way while keeping track of those around you.

Know What You Bring to the Team

To be effective on a team you have to know your own strengths and weaknesses and you need to join a team that can take good advantage of your skills. Additionally, look for teams that can compensate for your weaknesses. If you have never paddled a certain river or class of rivers, make sure you are with strong and experienced team members who can guide you through and bail you out if you get into trouble. Only by understanding yourself can you know how best to fit into the team.

On the other hand, if you are one of the most experienced paddlers, you need to make sure you have enough skill to handle rescues and other demands of the journey. You also need to have explicit conversations about such issues with the team leader and other team members before you plunge in. What do *you* want out of this trip? What will this trip require of you? What will you most need from others?

> To be effective on a team you have to know your own strengths and weaknesses and you need to join a team that can take good advantage of your skills. Additionally, look for teams that can compensate for your weaknesses.

Know Your Teammates

You also need to understand other members of your team, for at least three reasons. First, you might need their skills along the way, so you want to assess for yourself whether the team possesses the right skills to succeed. You can't necessarily rely on what anyone else, even the leader, might say about the team. If the team matters to you and to your success, then scout them before signing on to make the run with them. Even brief trips to the Internet or cursory conversations about whom they know, the type of work they've done, or what objectives they have for this project can yield useful information. You want to sign up with a group built to succeed and not with a poorly constructed one, likely to fail.

Second, and still more personal, the skills of team members could save your tail. The more fellow travelers on the river have skills in making this type of run, traveling this river, handling medical or rescue emergencies, managing logistics, or simply cooking, the more likely that you will stay safe, warm, well-fed, and in good health. In the office, you might have colleagues who have mastered the arts of virtual teaming, managing up, exotic and effective presentations, or project planning. These skills may not appear in their job descriptions; you have to draw the information out, and the sooner the better.

Third, you need to prepare for subteaming, breaking the larger group into smaller groups, even pairs. To design these informal sub-teams, like choosing teams in a pickup game of basketball, you have to know the strengths and weaknesses, virtues and vices of other team members before the call goes out to form a subteam or to buddy-up. Make sure that you end up with somebody who can and will keep an eye on and out for you. The world lacks an abundant supply of such people, hence the benefit of determining candidates early: better to surmise a person's value in advance than to discover any of their acute limits just when you need the person most.

Naturally, changes in the team or in the journey may require revisiting all these issues. Do you still want to belong? Have the mission or the competencies of the team changed so much as to jeopardize successfully completing this run of this river? For instance, what does it mean if the strongest paddler drops out just before the trip? When Tracy made the leap to the entrepreneurial company, she looked forward to working with the CEO and founder. But he sold the company just as she signed on and soon left the organization altogether. She felt abandoned and worried as she drove to work that first day. She already was headed down-stream, but her new team of paddlers was less experienced. She valiantly paddled on, but she eventually saw that this new config-uration of a team did not satisfy her expectations or her needs, so she negotiated for another team on another river.

> **You also need to understand other members of your team.**

Become Skilled at Entering and Leaving Teams

In permanent whitewater, even so-called permanent teams often turn out to be temporary. Individuals assemble to form temporary project or work teams. Much work occurs in parallel or in pockets along the river as individuals make their own way through their tasks, plying their individual skills while separated by miles or continents. Situations may demand interaction as may emergencies or key points of intersection. A larger authority and organizational context may dictate certain constraints, rules, processes, and scripts, but these seldom dominate the day-to-day passage down the river.

Trips, like projects, vary in complexity, difficulty, and in length. Traveling the Grand Canyon, for example, entails at least months of planning and weeks of execution. Other groups of paddlers form a few days in advance through the use of real or virtual mes-sage boards, cell phones, and the Internet. Some groups form at the riverside as kayakers congregate, drawn to the day or condi-tions on the river like earthworms after a heavy rain. People show up with boats at a popular river during release day and arrange to run "shuttles" (leaving cars at the takeout so they have a way to get off the river) and look for others with whom to make a run. They often know each other or have mutual friends so they have or can get a sense of one another and their abilities. But sometimes they have to rely on self-reports of others about their experience.

Companies in permanent whitewater hunger for folks who have the skills to arrange complex, planned project teams and quick-hit strike teams. They can form dynamic teams from the set of potential team members on the side of the river. They possess the leadership skills discussed in Chapter 9, "Leading Trips: Guiding Through Permanent Whitewater."

Gather before the trip or before setting out on a project. Do real work when you gather. Introduce yourselves and what you bring to "the party." Plan the trip. Lay out objectives. Assign roles. Discuss and agree on values and rules of the road. Develop responsibility charts for the most likely emergencies. Perhaps even name the group or the expedition. Join with people in creating a sense of camaraderie, direction, and organization.

So much of creating and sustaining teams lies, of course, in communication. Communication, in turn, requires both willingness and technique. To marshal the willingness, think of the consequences to one and all of a fractured and contentious group versus a cohesive and mutually supportive group. Next, think entropy: All systems, including human systems, require the input of energy or they wind down. You as a group member control whether to invest energy or to put that burden on others.

As for technique, recall again the advantages of active listening, a basic and powerful approach to all human interaction. Perhaps more basic still: Stay in touch. The medium does not matter—list-serves, Web cams, conference calls, temporary Web sites, group planning software. The message does matter—"We are a group that has and does work together." People forget, so revisit and refine plans. Keep the discussion of "what, how, and who" alive and under review. Use any signs of an issue, discovery, or refinement as a possible occasion to gather, at least telephonically if not physically. Keep it up on the river. Meet as a whole group to maintain the sense of the group as a whole. Review the day ahead and the day passed. Share experiences and plans face to face to deepen relationships as well as to prepare for "game" change as required. Debrief. Teams get better when they learn. They learn better when they process. They process better when they practice.

> Gather before the trip or before setting out on a project. Do real work when you gather. Introduce yourselves and what you bring to "the party." Plan the trip. Lay out objectives. Assign roles. Discuss and agree on values and rules of the road.

Find Safety in Numbers

At the end of the day, as discussed in Chapter 5, "Personal Flotation: You Are Responsible for Your Own Security," you are responsible for your own safety. That is the baseline. Flip the kayak, and most likely your paddle and your skill bring you upright—or not. (Although Rob has watched his friend Aaron execute the amazing "Hand of God" technique. He paddles next to a flipped kayaker who has missed a roll, reaches across the bottom of the boat, grabs the far edge and flips it back upright, much to the surprise and delight of the paddler. But generally you cannot expect a *deus ex machina* to swoop in and save your tail.) You provide your first and best line of defense.

That said, never paddle alone. A team can substantially contribute to your safety and security. First, a group of boaters, like any herd, flock, or school offers protection to the other members of the group. But the protection differs from that provided by the structure of an ocean liner. Schools of fish can scatter when a predator attacks in a way that makes it much harder for the hunter to catch them than if they were alone. They disappear in an explosion of bubbles before reassembling to swim off. The team, even an ad hoc and short-term team, provides protection to its members.

Kayakers never travel alone or at least they shouldn't. One kayaker decided to run the Schuylkill River in Philadelphia at night by himself. Few would classify this stretch of the Schuylkill as challenging, as long as you know where the dams are. So going solo, even at night, did not qualify as outrageously risky. Still, truly going solo without even a loosely coupled team or network presents additional and unnecessary risk. In this case, he broke his paddle. He had to swim. Eventually, he climbed out of the river and tried to hitchhike to the Philadelphia Canoe Club. He cut quite a figure dressed in full, dripping paddling gear with his thumb out—at night, not far from a major metropolitan area. Not surprisingly, no cars stopped. Any rational person driving by probably assumed that he dropped in from another planet. In general, it is safer not to paddle alone.

Even a "company of one" needs a network around it to succeed. In ensuring the safety of the other members of the team, you have to look to your own safety first. From sitting through countless safety films on airlines, we all know the instruction to put on your own mask before helping others. You need to take care of yourself first, then look around and attend to the care of others. First, your own skills need to be in order. Study setting up teams, best practices for meetings, and access aides such as group software and videoconferencing. Also attend to your communication and emotional intelligence skills so that you can both better send and better receive amidst the din of the river and the demands of the day.

Second, when joining or building teams for permanent whitewater, look carefully at the rescue and survival skills of other potential team members. A skilled, calm teammate can render far more effective aid to someone stuck in a hole or pinned against a rock than can a fellow traveler struggling themselves to keep their wits about them. In organizations, we often see such skills as softer, perhaps less essential. But we all can probably think of times when the day was saved by a person who kept her head in an emergency or brought the team together when it was falling apart. Does a person have a demonstrated capacity to adjust, both to the demands of the river and the needs of others? Do they have sufficient skills and do they know themselves well enough to avoid trouble? Do they have the skills and the demonstrated willingness to help others who encounter trouble? Not every member of the team needs to have these skills, but you need a critical mass both to minimize the chance of disaster and to maximize the chance of ably handling whatever might challenge the team.

> Never paddle alone. A team can substantially contribute to your safety and security. First, a group of boaters, like any herd, flock, or school offers protection to the other members of the group.

Understand What Game You Are Playing

A team is not a team is not a team. Casually, we refer to "teams." Correspondingly, we act as if everyone knows what constitutes a good team. We sloppily refer to almost any grouping of people to perform a task as a team, and then we talk knowingly about what makes a good "team." In reality, the definition of "team" depends on the game being played.

A team of kayakers differs from a football team, which differs from an orchestra or jazz quartet. The teaming skills you need depend on the game you are playing.

Robert Keidel created a framework for distinguishing between different types of teams and understanding the skills you need for each.[2] He classifies teams based on their level of autonomy, control, and cooperation. He presents a triangle to define the space that teams can occupy. At one vertex sits autonomy (baseball or a recital), at another control (football or an orchestra), and at the third cooperation (basketball, soccer, field hockey, or jazz). Any team occupies a space within that triangle. Ideally, the way that team operates corresponds tightly with the demands of the game that it plays.

Each type of team is different and demands different teaming skills. A good recital or baseball team looks and acts differently than a good orchestral or football team or a good jazz or basketball team. One would not and should not confuse assembling and directing an orchestra with presenting a recital or staging a jazz concert.

To determine whether you have a good team (and how to improve your team), you need to know what game you are playing. Kayaking is loosely coupled, depending in large part on individual skills. Similarly, recitals depend on the quality of individual performances linked by the fact that they occur in the same room on the same day. Baseball is similarly loosely coupled. It celebrates the individual performer, indeed it celebrates individuality and individual initiative. The outcome depends heavily on individual performances, especially in the central, defining, and repeated confrontation between batter and pitcher. Any given play may require coordination of a few team members, but the team with the best individual players usually triumphs, regardless of their relations with one another. Babe Ruth and Lou Gehrig barely spoke to one another as the Yankees ruled the known baseball universe. Procuring the best players matters more than player relationships or ingenious game plans, hence the general manager and the players matter more than the manager. Players earn more than managers and baseball managers earn about one half as much as coaches in football or basketball.

An orchestral concert, like football, depends on role specialization, hierarchy, and game plans. One does not "do one's own thing." A script dominates. Regimentation characterizes the tempo, and tight control rules human interaction. Long practicing interludes provide time to perfect scripts. In football, pauses in the action after virtually every play offer frequent occasions to revisit the script and for the coach to realign players. The coach (the script writer or composer) and the coach's surrogate (the quarterback, script reader, or conductor) star. The team plans the work and works the plan.

Basketball, jazz, field hockey, or lacrosse demand a different form of teaming. They reward deep, spontaneous, free-flowing, improvisational interdependence. Players play, and coaches have limited opportunities during a game to intervene. The coach leads the process of the team, teaching technique and helping to keep the many key relationships in good working order, but has to rely on the team and its processes for its own real-time decision making and execution. Just as in jazz, it's all about mutual adjustment and flexibility in the moment. Biggest sin? Withholding help from a teammate, even for a moment. Why? Because the game is all about a shared, densely packed, free-flowing moment, not the individual or a tightly scripted role.

Most organizations face a particular type of game, as do most groups within them. Playing, hiring, leading, developing, planning, and coaching all look different depending on the game, hence best to excel at the main game. Nonetheless, while one game may dominate, every organization and team plays different games at different times. Sometimes in football the play comes apart, a so-called "broken play," and individuals play basketball, improvising on the spot: A quarterback scrambles, a receiver breaks his pattern, or offensive players become defensive players. Sometimes, basketball teams will run set plays, foregoing improvisation, in favor of a well-practiced subroutine that seems to hold promise against this particular opponent on this particular trip down the court. So too may a baseball team hone particular interdependencies like exchanges between the second baseman and shortstop or infielders cutting off throws from outfielders with or without a call from the catcher. They do so, because these game situations while relatively infrequent can significantly affect the outcome of a game, and they require close, even intimate understanding of the requirements of the play and the abilities of a given teammate or two. Playing a game well depends in no small part on knowing what game you need to play when.

While kayaking on the river, the game is largely autonomy or baseball except in emergencies when it's basketball. Ashore, life takes on more of a football aspect with scripted roles and a fairly regimented hierarchy. Hence, assembling the right team means carefully selecting individual players for their individual skills while making sure of two other aspects. First, the group must have enough expert helpers to ensure safety. Second, each member has to slip into harness on shore and play his part.

> A team is not a team is not a team.
> In reality, the definition of "team"
> depends on the game being played.

Choose the Right Vessel

A kayak is not the only way down a whitewater river. The choice of vessel on the river or organizational structure in permanent whitewater can affect the type of team that forms and, therefore, the requirements of team members. For example, you can run whitewater in a raft, which leads to more tightly controlled teamwork, more like football or an orchestra. The raft has a captain, and crew members support one another, perhaps in the context of a flotilla of rafts or other boats. Six people working independently on a raft would lead to chaos.

Kayakers, on the other hand, play baseball, tending for the most part to pilot and paddle their own vessels, with a leader who serves more as a baseball coach most of the time, necessarily leaving the game to the players, and occasionally as a basketball coach, working to maintain the necessary if limited interactions among his players. Only rarely would a kayak coach act like a football coach, designing and then calling a scripted play. This might occur, for example, when paddlers need to thread the needle to make a specific route through a difficult rapid.

Organizations have teams of various types, some relatively structured and hierarchal as well as some far more flexible and autonomous. The choice of the team will affect the course of the journey. Examine any team closely before joining. Is the team set up to play the right game? How well can the team play the game? Do you fit or would you turn out to be a baseball player on a football team? Would you be a soloist buried in the orchestra, or vice versa? Will you benefit from learning how to play this game this way? In short, give thought to choosing the type of team you join.

Sometimes your choice of a vessel depends on your experience. For example, if you have less experience, you might choose a vessel such as a raft or an organization with a strong captain to gain experience and understand the water before setting out on your own. You might learn to play in the relative safety of an orchestra before taking to the stage for a solo. In an organization, such assignments can prove particularly appropriate and valuable to more junior workers before they take on more independent and riskier assignments. Like Tracy, you might gain experience in a more stable organization first, experience that you can then apply in new ways in an entrepreneurial startup. Even skilled kayakers sometimes first venture onto a river in a raft. Doing so gives them a better opportunity to learn the river. Such an approach may also well serve the more risk averse. Remember that while you might have no choice about working in permanent whitewater, you can choose how you go downstream.

> A kayak is not the only way down the river. You can run whitewater in a raft, which requires more coordination among team members. Organizations have teams of various types, some relatively structured and hierarchal as well as some far more flexible and autonomous. The choice of the team will affect the course of the journey.

Understand the Working of Teams

As with our flocks of starlings, teams possess a life of their own beyond the impulses of the individual members. Any collective has its own dynamics, for better and for worse, even for good and evil, that can affect the actions of individual team members. Well-managed teams demonstrate the positive power of teams. The *Apollo* astronauts would never have reached the moon without the coordinated efforts of a huge and talented team. The *Apollo 13* astronauts, stranded in space after an equipment failure, would never have touched Earth again without their own expert teaming and the extraordinary efforts of a much larger but no less dedicated team on the ground.

Yet, teams have a darker side as well. Team Enron created a context that made accurate, thoughtful, ethical evaluation of the state of the organization all but impossible. Teams do not necessarily equal, let alone surpass, the sum of their individual members. More than 30 years ago, for example, Irving Janis studied one path that groups take to suboptimization, even to disaster, and termed it "Groupthink," a form of delusional, self reaffirming decision making marked by bobble-headed "yes men." As Janis noted, a group can actually reinforce and strengthen errors in perception and in judgment and lead to disastrous consequences such as the Bay of Pigs invasion during the Kennedy administration. Everyone sat in a room and nodded their heads that this was a good idea. It was not. In that case, however, the group then examined its operating and learned. They redesigned the way the team functioned and performed at a remarkably high, even spectacular level, during the subsequent Cuban Missile Crisis.

Teams, in other words, can benefit greatly from strong-minded yet collaborative members. As Michael Eisner reportedly said about his staff, "I'll trade 10 IQ points for a point of view." Or, as quoted in Chapter 6, George Patton said, "If everyone is thinking the same way, then someone isn't thinking." If you don't feel right about the rapid ahead, say something. This counsel takes on special import when a decision carries legal or moral consequences.

Successful entrepreneur and billionaire Jon Huntsman served in the Nixon White House just before the Watergate crisis brought down the administration. He nearly succumbed to groupthink, but he refused to engage in what became known as "dirty tricks" and left the White House. Huntsman emerged as one of the few unindicted prominent staffers. He trusted his instincts, kept his bearings, said "no" to power and his team, and moved on.

Teams can make doing the right thing difficult. Consider a chilling set of experiments by American psychologist Philip Zimbardo. In his famous experiments at Stanford University in the 1970s, he randomly assigned 24 students as either prisoners or guards in a mock prison in the basement of the university psychology building. The students quickly took on their assigned roles, and took them to extremes. One-third of the guards exhibited sadistic behavior. The prisoners, also randomly selected students, became passive and depressed. Context affects our individual actions. A turbulent environment may present extreme challenges that test your core. Think of the mountain climber who had to choose between cutting the rope of a teammate or dying with him. The environmental danger is real. So too is our response. Whom we choose as teammates matters. How we act in their midst matters. Or, to quote concentration camp survivor Viktor Frankl, "everything will become still worse unless each of us does his best."[3]

More recently, in *The Lucifer Effect: Understanding How Good People Turn Evil*, Zimbardo offers recommendations for maintaining balance in a crazy world, including admitting mistakes, being aware and responsible, recognizing you are both an individual and part of a group, rebelling against unjust authority, valuing independence as well as group acceptance, being aware that the present is temporary, and opposing unjust systems.[4] Teams can help you maintain your sanity in a crazy world. But if they make you crazier or bring out your demonic side, stanch the flow. If you cannot, then move on and find a new team.

> A group can actually reinforce and strengthen errors in perception and in judgment and lead to disastrous consequences. Team Enron created a context that made accurate, thoughtful, ethical evaluation of the state of the organization all but impossible.

THE POWER OF THE TEAM

Like flocks of starlings, ad hoc teams can do extraordinary things when called on to do so. With little central organization, teams can pull together in a few short seconds in ways that might imply days of planning. For example, Rob's trip reached the rapid called Hermit on the Colorado River. Guides had warned them that the rocks had shifted. A huge wave opened up partway down the rapid. This beast had flipped a 30-foot motor launch—a rare event, like tipping an elephant. The first raft, with the trip leader in it, went down as kayakers waited at the top or scouted the rapid. The raft hit the giant wave. It turned almost vertical. By some miracle, it didn't flip over, but did unceremoniously eject the two occupants. The ghost raft moved downstream without any crew.

With the trip leader underwater, one might think the rescue effort would have devolved into chaos. Not so. One of the kayakers still scouting on the shore saw what happened and began blowing his whistle to signal trouble. The kayakers at the top of the rapid knew something was wrong, but not what. Aaron, one of the strongest paddlers, took off downstream to help after quickly deputizing a few other people to lead the rest of the kayakers down. He paddled up to the empty raft, pulled his boat onto the back, took the oars and paddled it into an eddy at the bottom. Another raft made a hairpin turn into the eddy where the two paddlers had been dumped. With the wild whirlpools on the Grand Canyon, they were bobbing up and down like horses on a carousel before he fished them out. The remaining kayakers went in small groups, with mixed results, but eventually everyone ended up rescued at the bottom.

The rescue was self-organizing. Information was scarce. A sentry or scout had seen enough to make sufficient sense of the unexpected to signal. A series of sharp blasts on a whistle told the boaters upstream that something was wrong, but not much else. Roles flowed. The strongest and most experienced paddlers knew what to do. They jumped in first, and also looked out for the weaker members of the group. No grand plan guided this activity, no plays chalked out on the blackboard. Like a flock of starlings, the group morphed to fit the situation. A team like this truly shines in a crisis.

Forming and participating in ad hoc teams is a fact of life in permanent whitewater. You need to understand what you bring to the team and understand the skills of other team members. You also need to recognize and appreciate the dynamics of the team, recognizing that what might feel like uncoordinated movement could actually be the progress of a flock of starlings. As Tracy discovered, you may sometimes need to join and leave teams along the way. The teams may change. The travelers who join you on the river may change, but skills in teaming will always be important.

> Like flocks of starlings, ad hoc
> teams can do extraordinary things
> when called on to do so. With little
> central organization, teams can
> pull together in a few seconds
> to accomplish the complex
> and the demanding.

THE TAKEOUT

Permanent whitewater means more ad hoc teaming, so you need skill in creating, maintaining and participating in flexible, temporary teams.

CHAPTER 9

Leading Trips
Guiding Through Permanent Whitewater

The CEO's job is lonely and getting ever more difficult. When you take it to heart, it becomes your life, not just a job.

—*Andrea Jung, Chairman and CEO, Avon Products*

A young physician drafted during the Vietnam War asked his superior to put him in any specialty except orthopedics, a specialty in which he felt potentially dangerously under-skilled. Of course, the colonel assigned him to orthopedics at a base in Tennessee.

One of the first cases was a complicated spiral fracture. The patient's leg was a mess. The young doctor, the supposed expert, resigned himself only to try his best to honor his professional oath to "do no harm." Worried, he considered how he might avoid disaster. A considerably older staff sergeant named Reg assisted him. Reg asked if the doctor would mind if he set up the patient for the procedure. The doctor quickly agreed and scurried off to his office to review his medical texts and to collect himself. Reg appeared at the physician's office door and asked whether the doctor would like to inspect the patient. The doctor came in, examined the patient, and marveled at how skillfully Reg had "set up" the injured soldier.

The physician told Reg that he had done a great job preparing the patient. Reg then said, "You probably have a lot of things to do, doctor. Do you mind if I get started on the patient? I'll call you if I need any help." The doctor just said thanks and returned to his office. A subsequent inspection of the patient showed a remarkable clinical performance by Reg, one that far outstripped anything that the doctor might have done. Reg, it turned out, had been doing this work for more than 20 years. Reg came from the most modest of backgrounds, lacked formal education, and as an African-American living in mid-twentieth century America had most probably been the victim of numerous acts of prejudice. But he had intelligence, skill, and caring. The white doctor had formal education, intelligence, and caring, but not the skill. Reg offered his skill, and the physician knew talent when he saw it. From then on, Reg did nearly everything of consequence, and the doctor had an easy tour of duty, fulfilling his oath to avoid "doing harm." The formal leader stepped aside and let the follower lead, for the benefit of all.

> The doctor had the formal education, but not the skill. The staff sergeant had intelligence, skill, and caring. The formal leader stepped aside and let the follower lead, for the benefit of all.

LEADING IN PERMANENT WHITEWATER

The leader has an important, even vital, role in permanent whitewater, but it differs from the role of leader in more stable environments and more hierarchical organizations. Leader and follower constantly shift and realign their working relationship in turbulence. Leaders in permanent whitewater need to adjust more and faster to an often rapidly and continuously changing reality to ensure the success of the expedition and the safety of the team. Consequently, leading through permanent whitewater requires flexibility, humility, and, paradoxically, the willingness to follow.

> # Leading through permanent whitewater requires flexibility, humility, and, paradoxically, the willingness to follow.

Understand Power and Influence on the River

Leaders anywhere and anytime can draw upon two types of power, namely, positional and personal. Positional power, as the name implies, comes with the title or rank and the position. Position affords at least a degree of legitimacy and access to various rewards and punishments as well as information. Vassals bow before kings because the king sits upon a throne, literally and figuratively. A dethroned monarch often lacks both a throne and a head. Followers defer to a country's president or company's CEO because of the positions they hold.

Personal power, on the other hand, flows from one's expertise and appeal. Over time, all leaders benefit from developing and drawing on personal power as often as possible, especially in routine tasks. They benefit because, day to day, followers prefer it; they find the exercise of such power less irritating. Whitewater makes personal power more important in part because positions change rapidly. Temporary, ad hoc team members frequently offer a leader far less positional power than ocean liner crews provide their designated leaders.

Even a leader vested with positional power should seek to migrate to personal power as rapidly as possible. Chaotic environments make this all the more important. The story of Wagner Dodge and the Mann Gulch fire, recounted powerfully in Michael Useem's *The Leadership Moment*, tragically illustrates the dangers of a leader trying to exercise positional power in the absence of personal power.[1] Wagner Dodge led an ad hoc team of fire fighters into the wilderness. Dodge had positional power. He also had a wealth of experience, a potential source of personal power. A man of few words, he chose not to spend time sharing this experience with his men, many of whom he met for the first time as they set out. He had time before boarding the transport plane, on the plane, or on the ground after arrival to connect with his temporary, young, and inexperienced charges. He chose not to discover their expertise or to disclose his own. He failed to demonstrate his experience to these followers, and so failed to build the personal power that later he might have used to good effect.

Reality quickly overpowered planning. Things fell apart. The men found themselves in a futile race to outrun the fire that they had come to fight. In full flight, Wagner Dodge invented a new technique, an escape fire, a brilliant innovation that saved his own life. It could have saved his entire crew but they wouldn't follow him into it. He lit a fire and jumped in the midst of the ground it cleared. They had never seen or heard of this technique before because Dodge had just invented it, and they didn't trust him. They thought him crazy. One declared, "To hell with that, I'm getting out of here!" Thirteen of the fifteen team members who rushed by their leader burned to death. Dodge and two others survived. Rank and position can mean little when making split-second, life-and-death decisions. In the crisis, Dodge didn't have the personal power he needed.

Permanent whitewater more often throws more crises at individuals and teams than do more stable environments. Hence, developing personal power takes on even greater importance. The leader of the team decides when to start, where to stop for lunch, where to take out, where to camp, and how to pace the journey if it is a multiday trip. The handling of these tasks provides the opportunity to move beyond limited positional power to personal power, the power needed in an emergency.

Leaders can gain personal power by building skills in all the areas discussed in the preceding chapters of the book, including creativity and optimism. The stark reality for leaders in permanent whitewater boils down to the following: A leader of a temporary group facing whitewater needs to develop personal power to lead effectively. Recall the tale in Chapter 6, "Scouting and Portaging: Set Your Own Course," of Lewis and Clark at the juncture of the Maria and Missouri rivers. Lewis and Clark had positional power, albeit somewhat limited by their circumstance. Their commitment to developing and using personal power prior to as well as in that moment helped both them and their followers to navigate a fundamental disagreement about, literally, which way to go.

The tale of a new commander at a fire base in the middle of nowhere during the Vietnam War offers a poignant example of what can happen if leaders facing prolonged demanding times do not go beyond positional power. In the midst of North Vietnamese troops, the base faced constant threat, held at bay only by a defensible location, the vigilance of its occupants, and the protection of American aircraft and artillery. Two problems persisted: snipers and water. Regarding the snipers, the troopers kept their own on watch to dissuade enemy snipers. Soldiers demurred from saluting officers to avoid disclosing such prime targets. As for water, no location proves perfect, and this location, while defensible, offered limited fresh water. Hence, the defenders journeyed to the river as needed, but anyone making that trip became much more vulnerable to attack.

Accordingly, the American troops took actions to limit consumption of water. They shaved every few days rather than every day. They wore sandals rather than combat boots and cut off the trousers of their fatigues to allow easier inspection for jungle rot and thereby less bathing. Consuming less water meant less risk for base occupants, however "irregular" they appeared.

A new commander arrived and promptly used positional power to enforce Army rules and regulations. Troops were to shave daily and only wear official Army clothing, no more sandals and no more field capris. Soldiers attempted for a week to educate the colonel about the error of his ways. They failed to convince him. They then went by the book and only by the book, including saluting their CO unfailingly, in plain sight of the snipers. In fact, soldiers went out of their way to find him and salute. Another week or so passed and a terrorized and twitching colonel boarded a helicopter never to return. He had positional power and tried to assert it in the absence of personal power. Surrounded by a truly hostile environment, rife with snipers, he quickly learned the liability of relying so heavily on positional power.

> The stark reality for leaders in permanent whitewater boils down to the following: A leader of a temporary group facing whitewater needs to develop personal power to lead effectively.

Build Trust

Leaders need to build trust quickly. Greg recalls a scene on a dory trip down the Grand Canyon where one of the junior members of the expedition staff capsized a raft in a major rapid. Other voyagers watched from dories up- and downriver. All strained to determine the state of the former occupants of the raft and what needed doing next. Was the dot pinned next to the boulder human or flotsam? Above the roar of the river, people "dialogued." Actually, they shouted at one another. It takes a certain level of trust to engage in such heated argument, especially for people who, as absolute strangers, had met but a few days before. Now, they debated what they saw and what to do—heatedly. They needed to do so, and the people in the river needed them to get it right and fast.

In more stable times, such trust flowed more easily. At the Henry Ford museum, regular demonstrations of the early days of baseball (pre-1900) reveal how much our whitewater world differs from the more genteel world of more than a century ago. The old game had only one umpire in contrast to four today. This meant that even the sharpest umpire would miss a lot, so umpires had to trust players. On a close play, the umpire would ask the player, "Sir, on your honor as a gentleman were you out or safe?" All present expected an honest report, whether the gentleman in question benefited from the honesty or not. Our permanent whitewater world changes too quickly for position and formality to cover all or even most exigencies. Relationships need to carry the day. Relationships turn on trust, and in whitewater, trust needs to form quickly.

We live in a paradoxical time. People increasingly depend more on ever more transitory team relationships. We assemble temporarily and work intensely, but for a short period of time. Like paddlers on a river, we depend on each other for safe transit even though we might have only recently met. As the authors of *Primal Leadership* write, "In an era when more and more work is done long distance—by e-mail or by phone—relationship building, paradoxically, becomes more crucial than ever."[2] Trust is more important, but it takes more effort and attention to build it. Building trust is one of the central tasks of leaders in creating and leading teams.

> Our permanent whitewater world changes too quickly for position and formality to cover all or even most exigencies. Relationships need to carry the day. Relationships turn on trust, and in whitewater, trust needs to form quickly.

Stepping Aside: Manage Shifting Roles

A person might lead for a trip, a task, a day, or a moment. Regardless, a new river and a new team may well present different challenges and require still different adaptation. Given these fluid roles, leaders develop finely tuned signals to enable followers to step up or to line up as appropriate to the task at hand. Enabling followers can turn on a leader's technique. For example, a leader can ask for input from the youngest, most junior person in the room to encourage participation, participation not constrained by hearing one's senior speak first. Similarly, leaders can signal that they want a flatter, blunter communication by their language. For example, a military leader might signal this openness by using a soldier's first name. The officer then signals a return to a hierarchical relationship by thanking the soldier for the comments. If the soldier doesn't take the cue, then the officer may thank the soldier again but more formally, reverting to calling the soldier by formal rank, such as "Thank you, Corporal Smith." Finally, if necessary, the officer will state, "We are done here, Corporal."

Any such technique requires at least two ingredients. First, the leader must succeed in conveying the personal legitimacy of the request. Restated, the follower must feel a certain humility from the leader, the humility that lends credibility to the request. The follower must feel that the leader believes that the follower can lead him or her to a better understanding or course of action. Second, the formal leader must honor the bluntness.

> A person might lead for a trip, a task, a day, or a moment. Given these fluid roles, leaders develop finely tuned signals to enable followers to step up or to line up as appropriate to the task at hand.

ROLE OF THE TRIP LEADER

Among the roles of trip leaders on whitewater trips are:

- Identifying the right people and drawing them together for the run. Do the members have the right skills for the level of challenge in the environment? Is there a good mix of different experience levels and skills?

- Organizing the trip, deciding where to put in and take out, and laying out the plan of travel, recognizing that this plan will change.

- Ensuring the safety of the party. The trip leader has responsibility for the safety of the group. This means understanding the potential hazards, providing rescue equipment, and ensuring that members who are new to this river know what is coming ahead.

- Defining the line. The trip leader will often define a clear passage through a rapid that others can follow (or sometimes designate someone else to lead the way). This doesn't mean that every member of the party will follow this exact line, and their experiences along the way can differ significantly. One may have a smooth passage while the next one following the same line may navigate the entire rapid upside down.

Similarly, in organizations, team leaders need to determine the composition of the team, organize the tasks and deadlines, and look out for the party along the way to protect them from organizational demands that might undermine the team. Leaders need to work without adequate formal authority, defining the line but not dictating it.

Enabling Leaders and Following Followers: Stepping Up to Leadership

People in our culture often virulently resist the tag of "follower" because they see it as a passive role. During a discussion of followership with a senior management team, a CFO interrupted forcefully to declare, "We are not sheep." He saw followers as sheep. As a people, we subscribe to the philosophy that the view only changes for the lead sled dog. Or, in the words of fictional race car driver Ricky Bobby from *Talladega Nights*, "If you're not first, you're last." Followers in permanent whitewater are not sheep—far from it. Indeed, they cannot afford to be. They are simultaneously followers and adventurers, partners in the journey, and essential team members, struggling together through a wilderness. Followers in permanent whitewater make a conscious choice to follow. Organizations change, but individuals also make their own career changes that take them out of a particular organization or away from a particular leader.

The leader therefore needs to keep at least three points firmly in mind. First, do not try to lead without followers. If so tempted, however, think of the colonel at the fire base surrounded by snipers. If your followers do not protect your position as leader by watching your back, then you won't last long. Second, recognize that skilled followers literally run the place. Without Radar, the medical camp in *M*A*S*H* would have fallen apart. Third, the line separating follower from leader often blurs, especially in turbulent environments. The best followers can and do rise to the challenge of leadership, and the best leaders demonstrate the capacity to follow.

An able leader in permanent whitewater builds adaptability into a team. An adaptable team contains a number of people capable of leading if called on to do so. Kenneth Chenault, CEO of American Express said, "Anyone at any level can be a leader...can define reality and give hope."[3] We lead ourselves or we lead no one, and kayaking requires large quantities of individual self-leadership. Who follows and who leads may well need to shift depending on the situation at the moment.

A whitewater river often demands that followers lead not just themselves but others. Perhaps the group separates or the leader must concentrate on a rescue. In such times, sheep don't cut it. You want people who can step forward and lead. Frank Wild was a dedicated and dependable second in command to Ernest Shackleton on the *Endurance* expedition. But when Shackleton took a handful of expedition members off for months in search of rescue he left most of the party on Elephant Island in Wild's hands. Wild led them through months of isolated, cold, and hungry waiting.

When Shackleton selected men to join his expedition, he started with a core—aides to trust such as Wild. Wild, a longtime protégé, confidante, and eventual alter ego, then handled hiring for the expedition. He separated the applications into three stacks: mad, hopeless, and possible. The "possibles" met with Sir Ernest and experienced his intense, unique, and easily off-putting interviews, but only after Wild, Shackleton's trusted lieutenant, forwarded them. Shackleton then looked for hardiness and optimism, but he followed Wild's lead in whom to consider.

Famed polar explorer Roald Amundsen similarly depended on Oscar Wisting. Over 16 years the two journeyed together, literally to the ends of the earth. (The two men shared the unique distinction of reaching both the North and South Poles.) Wisting repeatedly proved an indispensible team member, in part because of his ability to step forward into a wide variety of roles, including dentist, dog sledder, and ship's captain. When Amundsen abandoned his multiyear Arctic expedition on the *Maud* midway through to pursue aviation, he left Wisting in charge of completing the mission. Wisting proved more than up to the task. Wild and Wisting were dedicated followers, but when the moment called for it, they stepped forward to lead ably.

> Followers in permanent whitewater are not sheep—far from it. Indeed, they cannot afford to be. They are simultaneously followers and adventurers, partners in the journey, and essential team members, struggling together through a wilderness. And they often have to step up to leadership.

Assembling the Right Team

Leading starts with selecting the group for the run. Often, the issue does not come down to finding the willing, but rather sorting through the willing to find the able and, frankly, the desirable. Few of us would choose to spend time continually rescuing someone or wincing whenever one or more fellow travelers came into view. Hence, staffing this ad hoc, temporary group influences heavily the success and nature of the trip for you and for others. What combination of strengths and weaknesses should the group possess to make likely a successful, safe, and, yes, fun run?

Leading means finding that right combination of people for the task at hand and pushing back, even refusing to travel if the group seems unfit. Otherwise, the work will suffer. Well being will also suffer—yours and others'. Finally, your reputation will suffer, and in an ad hoc, network-based world, your reputation amounts, as noted earlier, to your lifeline.

As discussed in Chapter 8, "Building Flocks: Teaming for Today's Run," choosing the right team depends on what game you are playing. Playing successful baseball depends especially highly on the quality of the individual players. In fact, in baseball one can predict 80 percent of a team's performance by knowing individual performance statistics versus about 20 percent for a basketball team. For a leader, this means a special emphasis on procuring the right individuals. The general manager has much more to do with the success of a baseball team, therefore, than does the field manager, and the leader of a whitewater expedition needs to pay especially close attention to the work of a general manager—that is, procuring and retaining top individual performers.

Baseball Hall of Fame manager Earl Weaver said that the manager's job does not center on great game plans, but on picking the right team members. "Everybody knows all the strategies. Nothing's changed in a hundred years." Rather, "a manager's job…is to select the best players for what he wants done." Weaver, the positional leader on the field, helped the general manager (his boss) to pick the right players, and in baseball, the right players count the most. As he said, "People say I've never had to manage a bad team...Well, that's the *point*."[4] Kayaking and life in the permanent whitewater of today put special emphasis on never having to manage a bad team. Musical scores and playbooks matter and so do team dynamics, but not so much. This is a recital. It's not orchestra. It's not jazz. It's baseball. Take the time to get the staffing right. The leader has no more important job.

> **Leading means finding that right combination of people for the task at hand and pushing back, even refusing to travel if the group seems unfit.**

Structuring the Team

The leader's job does not end with selecting the right players. About a half century ago, the Ohio State studies, one of the first large-scale formal studies of leadership, identified the crucial role that leaders need to play in getting the structure of their teams right. Setting up the right players to play the wrong game or assigning them to the wrong positions can waste their skills. On the other hand, as one of Earl Weaver's players said of him, "The man's a genius at finding situations where an average player—like me—can look like a star because a lot of subtle factors are working in your favor."

Deciding the right size for the team exemplifies one such ongoing choice for a leader. Situational demands may require splitting a larger group into smaller groups of six to ten people. Perhaps the river makes even loose, baseball coordination of the large group too difficult, or perhaps junior members have demonstrated sufficient skill to warrant expanded responsibilities, or the leader needs to free him- or herself of the group to scout ahead. The leader may need to change the game, for the river may require tighter, more coordinated decision making for the sake of safety. The leader needs to set the size of the basic group right for the situation. Leaders may need to split the group into smaller subgroups along the way. Splitting a group on the river parallels splitting a group in organizational whitewater—split along the right lines or pay the price.

On the river, decision rules include the right mix of experienced and inexperienced paddlers to protect expedition members, to disseminate skills, or to honor personal style such as different paddling speeds. One group might like to take long, luxurious runs while another prefers to barrel down to the next takeout point. Separating kayakers based on preference ensures that they don't unnecessarily irritate one another from dawn to dusk. Assembling and reassembling teams requires attention to the river and to team members.

> The leader's job does not end with selecting the right players. Leaders need to decide on the right size and structure for the team.

HUMILITY AND THE ART OF LEADING FROM BEHIND

South African leader and Nobel Prize winner Nelson Mandela, recalling herding cattle in his youth, talks about the need to lead from behind. "It is better to lead from behind and to put others in front, especially when you celebrate victory when nice things occur. You take the front line when there is danger. Then people will appreciate your leadership."[5] He spent more than two decades in prison and led his nation out of the apartheid era. He understood danger. He also understood the complexities of leadership in an environment of turbulence and change. Jim Collins describes the balance between drive for success and personal humility as "Level 5 leadership."[6]

Above all in a turbulent environment, keep your humility, whether you lead the team or serve as a member of it. The Greeks believed that before the gods destroyed someone they first made him mad ("insane" in the parlance of our day). The Celts had a characteristically more sardonic view: Before the gods destroyed someone they first made him proud. Pride enhanced destruction in at least two ways. First, it cuts one off—from reality, from relationships, and thereby from learning. Being cut off allows one delusions, including of grandeur. Second, delusional pride makes the reality of destruction hurt more.

In whitewater, pride goeth before the crash. Successful kayaking is nothing if not reality based; little room exists for delusions of grandeur or sloppy reconnaissance. Whitewater kayaking amounts to an individual activity conducted in the presence, and with the support, of others not unlike life itself. "Flying solo" converts a challenging activity into an unnecessarily dangerous one. Yet a balance exists between being on your own and orchestrating a larger group. Consider this quote from a product director: "I'm a company of one—I have no team, no power; I share people with other projects. I can't tell people what to do—but I can convince them by appealing to their agenda."[7] Today, many managers find themselves "matricized"—increasingly dependent on ever more ad hoc and far-flung teams. Terrorizing? Perhaps. Paralyzing? Possibly. Intimidating? Probably. Humbling? Hopefully. Challenging? At the very least. Also, rewarding.

Or, more mundanely, consider Earl Weaver once again. People had filled Baltimore's Memorial Stadium for Brooks Robinson Day, a day set aside to honor the most beloved player in franchise history. Earl Weaver, Brooks' former manager or positional boss, worked his way to the microphone. The raspy voiced, hard-bitten, diminutive firebrand came closer to tears than any other speaker. He spoke as a leader to a great and empowering follower. He spoke of the first time that he gave the then already-great Brooks Robinson a sign (an order) and of how Weaver had wondered whether Robinson would follow it, and of how he'd "wondered every time since." He thanked Robinson for saving his job, "several times over the years." Then, in front of a silent, now somewhat confused and uneasy capacity crowd, Weaver said to this so-called follower, this accomplished, heralded, and dedicated professional, "Thank you, Brooks. Thank you a million times."[8] Earl Weaver, the leader, stopped speaking, moved away from the microphone, and left center stage to his follower...in truth and in humility. Nelson Mandela would have understood.

> In a turbulent environment, keep your humility, whether you lead the team or serve as a member of it.

THE TAKEOUT

Leading in permanent whitewater requires flexibility and humility, skill in building trust, selecting the team, and preparing followers to lead at any moment.

Conclusion, What Conclusion?

There are moments when everything goes well, but don't be frightened.

—*Jules Renard*

After hearing about "permanent whitewater" in one of Greg's programs, one executive took the metaphor to heart, as noted in Chapter 7, "Rising Above the Roar: Communicate Through Symbols." He decided to find a way to keep the idea front and center when he returned to his office. On a huge, multiple-panel flat screen TV in his company lobby, he played a continuous loop of an image of whitewater rafting. Some companies might have peaceful, bubbling New Age fountains. Not this one. He didn't want anyone in his organization to forget where they were. He didn't want them to be fooled by the serenity of a typical corporate office. They were up to their ears in rapids. He wanted them to feel it, see it, and to thrive in their real job, namely change.

Like the looping video, the whitewater never ends. In McHenry, Maryland, there is a manmade whitewater park. The Adventure Sports Center International (ASCI) park has rapids that can be made more difficult or easier with the flip of a switch. Some of the rocks even have bladders attached to them that can be filled or deflated to change the shape and difficulty of the rapid. At the end of the run a conveyor belt takes paddlers back up to the top. Purists may find this all a bit too civilized and controlled, but it illustrates a basic fact of life in our permanent whitewater environment, namely the voyage doesn't end. No steady state here; no steady state, change, steady state; rather every trip down the rapids leads to another trip. To those who like the pounding excitement of whitewater living and working, this endless cycle might feel like paradise. Those who do not favor such a world will feel uncomfortably akin to Sisyphus, the king in Greek mythology condemned to roll a boulder up the hill every day, only to have it roll back to the bottom. Each morning, he started over again.

A whitewater paddler, however, would see a different world, a far more engaging and intriguing world. As discussed in the previous chapters, the whitewater kayaker views the world differently than the sailor on the ocean liner. Instead of looking to the organization to provide a sane pace, in whitewater you have to pace yourself. Instead of avoiding failure, you have to prepare to fail gracefully and learn to recover quickly. Paddlers look for places to play and move forward with a sense of optimism. Sailors derive their security from the mother ship, but in whitewater you need to look after your own security, relying on a portfolio of skills for personal flotation. The ocean liner's captain sets course from the bridge, but as a paddler you need to learn to read and react, scouting and portaging as you make your way down the river. In the tumult of permanent whitewater, you need to communicate through actions, symbols, stories, and myth because the environment drowns out traditional communications. You recognize that the organizational chart offers only rough guidance. On a whitewater river, position matters less than the skills in creating, leading, and joining teams for the day's run.

These skills, together with a shift in mindset, should transform your view of the environment and increase your chances of surviving—and even thriving—in this environment. This permanent whitewater world need not turn your life into a modern version of the hopeless tale of Sisyphus or a version of the tragic, topsy-turvy world of the *Poseidon Adventure*. Rather, you can emulate the valiant one-armed John Wesley Powell making his way down the Grand Canyon for the first time or follow the example of Lewis and Clark on their journey of discovery. Permanent whitewater demands more but can draw out the best from us, so long as we can recognize fully that our real job is change and learn to thrive at it.

BUILDING THE G-RIG

The right equipment and mindset make all the difference. After Powell made his pioneering journey through the Grand Canyon, few followed, a mere 100 more in the subsequent 80 years. They considered it a journey only for the hardy—or foolhardy. The Powells of the world, with the reflexes and fortitude to battle the river with primitive vessels, were (and are) few and far between.

Then Georgie White Clark came along and opened the Canyon to thousands of visitors every year. She didn't start out to transform Grand Canyon travel. She was just passionate about outdoor sports. In 1936, she rode across the United States by bicycle. She did mountain climbing and skiing. She plunged into the Colorado River, swimming the Canyon in 1945, wearing only a swimsuit, sneakers, and a life jacket. In 1947, she became one of the first people to take an inflatable raft down the Grand Canyon, and in 1952 she became the first woman to row the full length of the Marble and Grand Canyons.

But Clark's greatest innovation was the G-rig, a more stable raft made from lashing three World War II surplus bridge pontoons together, with an outboard motor for steering. Using this new craft, and wanting to share the expenses with fellow passengers, she launched commercial tours of the Grand Canyon. Clark ran her tours for 45 years. In her seventies, she still piloted her raft, wearing a leopard-patterned bathing suit, holding the tiller in one hand and a beer in the other.

Powell's rugged followers, who pitted themselves against the elements in simple, open dories, viewed the new G-rig with contempt. They had made a virtue of what Powell had faced as a necessity. But Clark's new craft transformed Grand Canyon travel. The right equipment made it possible for ordinary people to navigate this extreme whitewater. The river had not changed (although dams have changed its complexion since Powell's time). The set of rapids had not changed. Yet, a deadly trip became a navigable passage. The right equipment and skills made all the difference.

In today's organizations, many of us find ourselves thrown into churning whitewater. We experience not just a difference in the speed and magnitude of change, but a qualitative difference in the dynamics of change. While this might appear obvious, very few of us have developed enduring, effective strategies for meeting the challenges presented by these dynamics. Even the courageous Powell would have benefited from the right skills and equipment for permanent whitewater. The skills and mindsets in the preceding chapters give you the equivalent of the G-rig or at least a modern kayak. The river will still churn just as white, the water feel just as cold and wet. The river may not change, but you can. You can gain the right orientation and skills to thrive in permanent whitewater.

THE RIVERS ARE RISING

Many of us started our careers or learned about business in more placid environments. When we noticed that the pace of change picked up, we might well have believed that "things" would settle down, that the cheese would stop moving...eventually. Yet, the organization you joined—or even the one you walked into this morning—may change significantly by the time you leave for the day. Permanent whitewater represents a new and, paradoxically, permanent environment.

If you are reading this book, you probably do not need convincing about the turbulence of the environment. But consider a few signs of the increasing *fluidity* of our world, of the nature of the streams that feed it, and of their depth. Consider questions such as when is this going to end?

Is all this temporary? Will the river, like the Colorado beyond the Grand Canyon, empty into a nice placid lake? Or, better yet, when will the ramps go down for loading the Queen Mary? Will we return to a steady state or even a steady state, change, steady state world? If we will, we can wait it out and then settle back into a crew race with strong head-to-head competition but in a calmer, quieter, more organized world. If not, then whitewater will continue as our reality. We will need kayaks, not sculls and not ocean liners, for many years to come.

For one convincing take on why permanent whitewater will continue, travel to YouTube and view any version of Karl Fisch's "Did You Know?" One quick example: The U.S. Department of Labor estimates that today's learner will have 10-14 jobs by the age of 38. Fisch, a Colorado teacher, notes that "We are currently preparing students for jobs that don't yet exist using technologies that haven't been invented to solve problems we don't even know are problems yet."[1]

Whitewater is here to stay. If anything the river is rising. From a business perspective, at least three major wellsprings feed the whitewater: globalization, capital markets, and technology. Globalization has many facets, evolving for centuries, derailed by two world wars and the Great Depression, and strongly accelerating since 1950. One trend captures the aspect of most interest here, namely the sustained rush and roil of economic flow. Since 1950, world GDP has grown steadily while exports as a percentage of world GDP has risen from about 8 percent to nearly 30 percent.

The value of both merchandise and commercial services exported has increased by about 50 percent in the last decade.

America welcomes more than one million people, 350,000 private vehicles, 62,000 trucks and containers, 600 ships, and 2,500 aircraft—*daily*. Our food now travels between 1,500 and 2,500 miles from farm to table, as much as 25 percent farther than two decades ago. We live in a global economy with all the benefits, vulnerabilities, and fluctuations that entails—ever faster flowing competition and associated change, day after day.

Capital markets, the second stream, grow bigger, faster, and more mobile than ever with international currency transactions topping more than one trillion dollars a day, or more than five times U.S. dollar or Swiss franc reserves, more than even the Japanese or Chinese cash reserves. Theoretically, the markets could topple any currency in, at most, a day. Besides volume, there's speed—information technology makes moving unprecedented amounts of capital faster and easier than ever. In 1970, two-thirds of the value of capital markets lived in the United States; now two-thirds lives outside. Huge amounts of capital search for ideas, for opportunity. Resources can (and do) appear in record amounts and at record speed. The river gains momentum even as the strength of competitive cross-currents grows.

Finally, technology feeds and agitates the river. Figure 1 shows the growth in patents granted in the United States over more than 200 years. The chart illustrates that technology is autocatalytic—feeds on itself. Each technological advance enables more advances. Some advances prove epic: A millennium or more of European experience and experimentation with tool-and-die techniques enabled Gutenberg to develop movable print and forever change the dissemination of knowledge. Many advances prove cumulative. They refine and eventually outdate earlier forms of the technology.

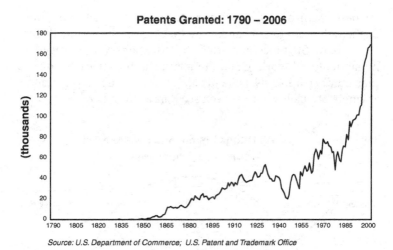

Patents Granted: 1790 – 2006

Source: U.S. Department of Commerce; U.S. Patent and Trademark Office

FIGURE 1   Technology, as seen in U.S. patents, is one of the streams contributing to permanent whitewater.

We have probably just begun our technological travels. Figure 2 demonstrates that we have only recently discovered that perhaps 96 percent of the "stuff" of the universe was beyond our sight; we literally did not know that it was there. That means most of what we have studied and know fairly well comprises only about 4 percent of the universe. No one can predict what this will mean, but it will unfold over the decades and lifetimes ahead, and it will add to the roll and roil of the river: new knowledge, new opportunities, new products, entirely new industries.

Beneath all of this lies an even more fundamental contributor to permanent whitewater: the rise of specialization. For tens of thousands of years, *Homo sapiens* spent virtually all of their "work" time dealing with fundamentals such as clothing, shelter, and especially, food. Animal domestication and early planting meant that around 10,000 years ago, 2 to 3 percent of the population began to specialize, igniting the rise of medicine, art, architecture, sciences, mathematics, and written language. Specialization drove further advances (and change). By the start of the twentieth century, about 80 percent of the United States was engaged in nonagricultural work. Computers and the Internet have driven that number up to 99 percent. No, Toto, we are not in Kansas anymore. Actually, we can't even see Kansas from here.

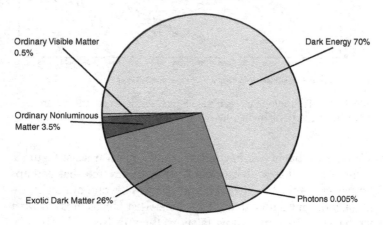

All Things Visible and Invisible
Composition of the Universe

Ordinary Visible Matter 0.5%

Dark Energy 70%

Ordinary Nonluminous Matter 3.5%

Exotic Dark Matter 26%

Photons 0.005%

Source: Paul Steinhardt, Scientific American

FIGURE 2 About 96 percent of the "stuff" of the universe is "out of sight."

In the process, one might describe our society as no longer one of specialists, but increasingly one of *subspecialists*. In the United States, Ph.D.'s increased 120-fold during the twentieth century. A similar change has occurred throughout the world (see Figure 3).

Having more Ph.D.'s indicates increased specialization or subspecialization. Physicians train longer with increasing numbers training beyond medical school. Marketers specialize by industry, niche market, and medium. Auto mechanics go to school full time for months before receiving certification.

Everybody's Doing It

Percent of total population enrolled in tertiary education for selected countries

	1970	1990s*	% female 1990s*
Brazil	0.44	1.17	52.9
Britian	1.08	3.25	51.8
China	0.01	0.49	33.3
France	1.58	3.54	54.9
India	0.44	0.65	36.2
Indonesia	0.20	1.16	34.8
Iran	0.26	0.91	38.1
Israel	1.86	3.59	51.3
Mexico	0.49	1.76	47.7
South Africa	0.37	1.49	48.0
South Korea	0.63	5.65	36.9
Turkey	0.48	2.35	35.1
United States	4.14	5.37	55.1

Most data from 1996. Some numbers from 1992, 1993, 1994, 1995, 1997.

Source: Economist, UNESCO, UNPO

FIGURE 3   Subspecialization is rising around the world.

Specialization and subspecialization increase whitewater and fragment reality, increasing the froth and foam. Part of a company (let alone part of a society or world) receives payment to narrow its focus, to specialize, to discover, to invent, and thereby to add more water to the river of change. Specialization pays for itself by generating the next advance and thereby feeding the currents of change. In effect, we live in a society organized to generate ever more change.

Specialization also fragments reality. People across specialties and particularly across subspecialties do not share the same reality. Our ancestors, Gork and Gak, on the sub-Saharan plains of East Africa 20,000 years ago did not, most probably, ever have to say "let me put this in context for you." We say that phrase or something like it multiple times every day. Gork and Gak shared a context: a fiery yellow ball moving across the sky, hunger, and a crucial need to avoid large, carnivorous animals. We share a fragmented, segmented, and subdivided reality of our own creation. This reality creates and amplifies the whitewater by renewing and creating anew obstacles and cross-currents.

Within organizations, this increasing fluidity and speed translates into an extremely complex and uncertain work environment. Surveys show that we live in the most prosperous time in history. We also live in a world of high-speed competition and stress. We chronically feel short of time (and in need of yet another guide to time management) and more frightened than ever (and in need of yet another type of anxiety or stress treatment). The percentage of U.S. workers who said they fear a layoff rose from 20 percent in 1990 to 37 percent in 1998.[2] Even in the white hot economy leading up to the tech bubble, note the churning in the economy (and people's lives!) represented by Figure 4.

An April 2001 survey found that 74 percent of workers were concerned about job security. About one-third of workers were "frequently concerned" about layoffs in 2005 (well into a period of economic expansion), the same as in 2001, amidst a recession. About 20 percent feared losing their job "soon."[3] Boom times seem as frightening as bust times.

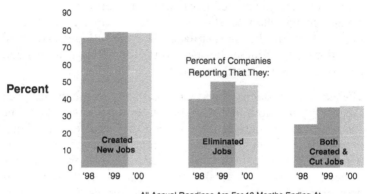

Figure: Downsizing and Upsizing: The Beat Goes On

Percent

Percent of Companies Reporting That They:

Created New Jobs — '98 '99 '00
Eliminated Jobs — '98 '99 '00
Both Created & Cut Jobs — '98 '99 '00

All Annual Readings Are For 12 Months Ending At MidYear. Categories Are Not Mutually Exclusive

Source: American Management Association

FIGURE 4   Churning waters lead to job churn.

NO PLACE TO HIDE—BUT WHY WOULD YOU WANT TO?

In this environment, some employees cling to (or crawl under) the few quiet rocks that they can find along the way. But there are fewer and fewer places to hide. Regulated industries? Government? Universities? Religious organizations? Not much peace and tranquility resides even in those traditionally stable sectors. The waters rise. You've already passed the last takeout before the rapids. So, hang on. Permanent whitewater has crept into every corner of the world. There is no dry place and few if any places to hide.

This environment can invoke anxiety, even fear. Late one day, a senior manager trying to empower employees in a large manufacturing complex summoned Greg, who was working with him on a major change effort, an effort precipitated by massive and ongoing changes in the marketplace. The executive clearly had something on his mind, but he wasn't talking. He hemmed and hawed. They waited for the elevator.

The executive suddenly asked Greg for his home phone number. "You're welcome to it, but why do you want it?" Greg asked. The executive looked down at the floor and then squarely into Greg's eyes: "So when I'm up pacing the floor at 2 a.m., wetting my pants, worrying about this place being out of control, I have someone to talk to." Listening to the roar and looking into the deep waves of a whitewater rapid can frighten us. Even the truly courageous and legitimately tough can feel fear. Yet, the river offers more than the occasion to fear. It offers challenge and opportunity alike. In this environment you can create what Mihaly Csikszentmihalyi calls "flow" in your life.[4] You give life meaning. You define your purpose. You define goals, and so "the meaning of life is meaning; whatever it is, wherever it comes from, a unified purpose is what gives meaning to life." Having created such a backdrop of purpose and goals, you have created the platform for your finest moments and fondest memories: "The best moments usually occur when a person's body or mind is stretched to its limits in a voluntary effort to accomplish something difficult or worthwhile." This is the challenge and opportunity of permanent whitewater.

The trip looks long and wet. Change dominates the world around you, but it need not dominate you. Your adjustment to it begins with appreciating that it exists. If you paddle about believing that you live in a steady-state world occasionally interrupted by change, then you mistake reality. You do so at your peril and at the peril of your fellow travelers.

Therefore, adopt a mindset of permanent whitewater. This metaphor can help you manage your own sanity effectively, beginning by recognizing reality and helping you to keep that reality where it belongs, namely outside yourself. Yes, the environment is crazy, but you can adjust. Hang up your sailor suit, grab your paddle and plunge in. Develop the set of mental and behavioral skills you need. No matter how rough the waters, you can develop the skills to meet them. Ahead stretch the rapids of permanent whitewater. Welcome to life on the river and fear not. Your real job is, and will most likely remain, change and you can master the mindset and the skills to handle that job. You can even thrive at it.

Endnotes

PREFACE

1. "Colorado River Use Statistics," Grand Canyon River Outfitters Association.
2. Peter Vaill introduced the term "permanent whitewater," which was the starting point or inspiration for this work, in *Managing as a Performing Art* (San Francisco: Jossey-Bass, 1989).
3. Spencer Johnson, *Who Moved My Cheese? An Amazing Way to Deal with Change in Your Work and in Your Life* (New York: G. P. Putnam's Sons, 1998).

CHAPTER 1

1. Fact Monster, "Titanic Facts," http://www.factmonster.com/spot/titanic.html.
2. In Canada and Greenland the term "Eskimo" has fallen out of favor, is considered pejorative, and has been generally replaced by the term "Inuit." However, while "Inuit" does correctly describe all of the Eskimo peoples in Canada and Greenland, that is not true in Alaska and Siberia. In Alaska the term "Eskimo" is commonly used because it includes both Yupik and Inupiat, while "Inuit" is not accepted as a

collective term or even specifically used for Inupiat (which technically is "Inuit"). To date, no universally acceptable replacement term for "Eskimo," inclusive of all Inuit and Yupik people, has achieved acceptance across the geographical area inhabited by the Inuit and Yupik peoples.

The primary reason "Eskimo" is considered derogatory is the false but widely held belief that it means "eaters of raw meat," which has an unappealing and deprecating ring to it. There are two somewhat different etymologies in available scientific literature for the term "Eskimo." The most well known comes from Ives Goddard at the Smithsonian Institution, who says it means "Snowshoe netters." Quebec linguist Jose Mailhot, who speaks Innu-Montagnais (which Mailhot and Goddard agree is the language from which the word originated), published a definitive study in 1978 stating that it means "people who speak a different language."

Nevertheless, while the word is not inherently pejorative, owing to folklore and derogatory usage, since the 1970s in Canada and Greenland "Eskimo" has widely been considered offensive. In government usage the term has been replaced overall by "Inuit." The preferred term in Canada's Central Arctic is "Inuinnaq," and in the eastern Canadian Arctic "Inuit." The language is often called Inuktitut, though other local designations are also used. The Inuit of Greenland refer to themselves as "Greenlanders" or, in their own language, "Kalaallit," and to their language as "Greenlandic" or "Kalaallisut." (http://en.wikipedia.org/wiki/Eskimo).

3. Note that in this book, we use the term "capsizing" as it is typically used in general conversation, to designate a boat overturning. While most people would consider a boat to capsize when it flips over, kayakers typically have a different view. They refer to capsizing only when the paddler actually swims. This subtle but significant distinction is an illustration

of the difference in mindset between kayakers and ordinary (some might say "sane") nonpaddlers. Only swimming is a problem. Flipping the boat is all in a day's work. For simplicity in this book, we use capsizing to refer to flipping the boat.

CHAPTER 2

1. Sylvia A. Hewlett and Carolyn B. Luce, "Extreme Jobs: The Dangerous Allure of the 70-Hour Workweek," *Harvard Business Review*, December 2006.

2. "Sleep Debt and Its Ravages," *BusinessWeek*, January 26, 2004.

3. Health-Disease Treatment WordPress blog, "Sleep Deprivation and Traffic Accidents," November 21, 2007, http://diseasetreatment.wordpress.com.

4. Martin Moore-Ede, *The Twenty-Four-Hour Society* (Reading, MA: Addison-Wesley, 1993), 5-8. (The Cumulative Sleep Deprivation graph... pg. 59).

5. Technological advances mean that we hold more power literally at our fingertips. Economically, more and more needs doing by fewer and fewer of us. For example, oil refineries and chemical plants continue to decrease the number of human beings they employ even as they increase production. Similar developments occur in other industries such as airlines and trucking. Martin Moore-Ede, *The Twenty-Four-Hour Society* (Reading, MA: Addison-Wesley, 1993), 6-7. Even the U.S. military has adopted doctrine to load more discretion and power deeper into the ranks (*Warfighting*, U.S. Marine Corps, 1989, 1997).

6. William J. Cromie, "Doctor Fatigue Hurting Patients," *Harvard Gazette*, December 10, 2006, http://www.news. harvard.edu/gazette/2006/12.14/99-fatigue.html.

7. "Multiple Risk Factor Intervention Trial (MRFIT)," *Harvard Men's Health Watch*, February 2006, 7. The protective effect of vacations remained valid after socioeconomic considerations and well-established cardiovascular risk factors were taken into account.

8. Tom Conger, "Combating Cognitive Overload," *Trend Letter*, August 2007, 8-9.

9. Gerald T. Lombardo and Henry Ehrlich, *Sleep to Save Your Life* (New York: HarperCollins, 2005), 35-49.

10. "Siestas and Your Health: Can You Nap Your Way To Health?" *Harvard Men's Health Watch*, January 2008, 7.

11. Joe Robinson, *Work to Live: The Guide to Getting a Life* (New York: Perigee, 2003).

12. *Trend Letter*, August 2007, 9; Families and Work Institute http://www.familiesandwork.org; and Expedia Travel Trendwatch, http://www.expediatraveltrendwatch.com.

13. *Trend Letter*, August 2007, 7.

CHAPTER 3

1. William R. Ferris, "Arthur Miller Interview," *Humanities*, March-April 2001, http://www.neh.gov/whoweare/miller/interview.html.

2. Paul Schoemaker and Robert Gunther, "The Wisdom of Deliberate Mistakes," *Harvard Business Review*, June 2006.

3. Edward Hallowell, *CrazyBusy: Overstretched, Overbooked, and About to Snap!* (New York: Ballantine Books, 2006).

CHAPTER 4

1. Stephen B. U'ren, *Performance Kayaking* (Harrisburg, PA: Stackpole Books, 1990), 142.

2. Martin Seligman, *Authentic Happiness* (New York: Free Press, 2002), 93-100.

3. Jerry Hirshberg, *The Creative Priority: Driving Innovative Business in the Real World* (New York: HarperCollins, 1998).

4. Daniel Pink, *A Whole New Mind: Why Right-Brainers Will Rule the Future* (New York: Berkeley Publishing, 2005), 66.

5. George Vaillant, *Aging Well* (Boston: Little, Brown and Co., 2002), 310-311.

6. Betty Friedan, *The Fountain of Age* (New York: Touchstone, 1994).

7. Kay Redfield Jamison, *Exuberance: The Passion for Life* (New York: Alfred A. Knopf, 2004), 4-6.

8. Robin Gerber, *Katherine Graham: The Leadership Journey of an American Icon* (New York: Penguin Group, 2005), 207.

CHAPTER 5

1. Roald Amundsen, *My Life As An Explorer* (New York: Doubleday, 1927), 236-237.

2. Kathleen Flinn, *The Sharper Your Knife, the Less You Cry: Love, Laughter, and Tears at the World's Most Famous Cooking School* (New York: Viking, 2007); http://www.kathleenflinn. com.

3. Tom Peters, "The Brand Called You," *Fast Company 10*, August 1997, 83; Cliff Hakim, *We Are All Self-Employed: The New Social Contract for Working in a Changed World* (San Francisco: Berrett-Koehler, 1994); Peter Cappelli, *The New Deal at Work: Managing the Market-Driven Workplace* (Boston: Harvard Business School Press, 1999); William Bridges, *JobShift: How To Prosper in a Workplace Without Jobs* (New York: Perseus Books, 1994); William Bridges, *Creating You & Co.: Learn to Think Like the CEO of Your Own Career* (New York: Perseus Books, 1997).

4. Manpower, Inc., Web site, "About Manpower: Who We Are," http://www.us.manpower.com.

5. Ibid.

6. Daniel Pink, *Free Agent Nation: The Future of Working for Yourself* (New York: Warner Books, 2001), 17.

7. Frederick P. Brooks Jr., *The Mythical Man-Month* (Reading, MA: Addison Wesley Longman, 1995) and Robert J. Graham, *Project Management as If People Mattered* (Bala Cynwyd, PA: Primavera Press, 1989). Study Larry Hirschhorn, *Managing in the New Team Environment* (Reading PA: Addison Wesley Longman, 1991), paying special attention to Chapter 5, "Taking the Learner Role," which lays out the challenge, opportunity, and orientation to assist in managing our need for control in the service of learning, especially learning as we go.

8. CFAR (Center For Applied Research) of Philadelphia and Boston can provide valuable assistance here. www.cfar.com

9. Wharton has a particularly good negotiations program run by G. Richard Shell and colleagues. Wherever you go, make sure that the course provides multiple and prolonged opportunities to negotiate and to debrief. Negotiation is a skill best learned by doing and doing and doing. Practice or pay. That said, get familiar with G. Richard Shell's *Bargaining for Advantage: Negotiation for Reasonable People* (New York: Viking, 1999). As for the related skill of persuasion, look to sources such as Kerry Patterson et al. in *Crucial Conversations: Tools for Talking When Stakes Are High* (New York: McGraw-Hill, 2002) and their *Crucial Confrontations* (New York: McGraw-Hill, 2005), and G. Richard Shell and Mario Moussa's *The Art of Woo: Using Strategic Persuasion to Sell Your Ideas* (New York: Penguin, 2007).

10. Bruce McEwen, *The End of Stress as We Know It* (Washington, DC: Dana Press, 2002).

11. *Ibid.*, 16.

12. *Ibid.*, 149.

13. Christopher Wills, *Children of Prometheus: The Accelerating Pace of Human Evolution* (New York: Perseus Books, 1998).

14. Older works, such as Morgan W. McCall, Jr., Michael M. Lombardo, and Ann M. Morrison, *The Lessons of Experience* (New York: Lexington Books, 1988), or newer works, such as Marshall Goldsmith, *What Got You Here Won't Get You There* (New York: Hyperion, 2007), all stress the ongoing nature of professional development. At one level, this point comes as no surprise. After all, Jung, Erickson, and Levinson among others have long discussed the broader psychological and emotional work that occupies us throughout our lives. We change from the inside out as we age, even as our whitewater world continues to change the skills it demands.

    The skills matter, to be sure. Michael M. Lombardo and Robert W. Eichinger's *Eighty-Eight Assignments for Development in Place* (Center for Creative Leadership, 1989) remains a most useful outline for delineating work challenges and how to develop skills for handling them. Their more recent compilation of key work competencies, performance dimensions, and key career stallers and stoppers also details approaches to targeted development (*For Your Improvement,* third edition (Minneapolis: Lominger Limited, 2003)). Clarifying your development needs (often through careful listening) leads to concentrating on timely, beneficial skill improvement.

15. Mark S. Granovetter demonstrated in 1974 the key role that contacts played in a person getting work and developing a career in *Getting a Job: A Study of Contacts and Careers* (Chicago: University of Chicago Press, 1974).

16. "Playing in the Dirt To Counter Depression," *Medical Research News*, April 2, 2007, http://www.news-medical. net/?id=22805.

CHAPTER 6

1. Outside Online, "Liquid Thunder," http://outside.away. com/tsangpo/liquid_thunder_4.html.

2. Ibid.

3. Peter Teeley and Phillip Bashe, *Cancer Survival Guide* (New York: Broadway Books, 2005).

4. Hasbro Web site, "Over 110 Years of Fun: The Story of Parker Brothers," http://www.hasbro.com/default. cfm?page=ci_history_pb.

5. Pick the book—*Resonant Leadership, Emotional Intelligence at Work, What Got You Here Won't Get You There, The Art of Woo*, or *Micromessaging*—and communication generally and listening specifically figures centrally. Find and read the classic article "Active Listening" by Carl Rogers and Richard Farson. Then practice, practice, practice. You do not have time to learn the river all by yourself. Paradoxically, to travel on your own, prepare regularly with others.

6. Wikipedia defines life coaching as "a practice of helping clients determine and achieve personal goals. Life coaches use multiple methods to help clients with the process of setting and reaching goals. Coaching is not targeted at psychological illness, and coaches are not therapists or consultants." Jim Naughton of *Psychotherapy Newsletter* equates them to "personal trainers" (*USA Today*, August 4, 2002, http:// usatoday.com).

7. America's Story from America's Library Web site, "Lewis and Clark and the Great Falls Portage," http://www. americaslibrary.gov/cgi-bin/page.cgi/aa/explorers/ lewisandclark/portage_3; Lewis & Clark Voyage of Rediscovery Web site, "Falls Left Lewis in Awe," John Krist, http://www.voyageofrediscovery.com/part7/trail/index.shtml.

8. University of Nebraska–Lincoln Web site, The Journals of the Lewis and Clark Expedition, June 2, 1805, http://libtextcenter.unl.edu/examples/servlet/transform/tamino/Library/lewisandclarkjournals?&_xmlsrc=http://libtextcenter.unl.edu/lewisandclark/files/xml/1805-06-02. xml&_xslsrc=http://libtextcenter.unl.edu/lewisandclark/LCstyles.xsl.

9. Christina Maslach and Susan E. Jackson, "The Measurement of Experienced Burnout," *Journal of Occupational Behavior*, vol. 2. no. 2, April 1981, 99-113.

10. Richard E. Boyatzis and Annie McKee, *Resonant Leadership: Renewing Yourself and Connecting with Others Through Mindfulness, Hope, and Compassion* (Boston: Harvard Business School Publishing, 2005), 54-55.

11. Bruce McEwen, *The End of Stress As We Know It* (Washington, DC: Dana Press, 2002), 10.

12. David F. Dinges, Ph.D., Chief of the Division of Sleep and Chronobiology at the University of Pennsylvania, presentation to Wharton AMP, July 2007.

13. Paul D. Walker, *The Cavalry Battle That Saved the Union* (Gretna, LA: Pelican Publishing, 2002); Thom Hatch, *Clashes of Cavalry* (Mechanicsburg, PA: Stackpole Books, 2001); Warren C. Robinson, *Jeb Stuart and the Confederate Defeat at Gettysburg* (Lincoln, NE: University of Nebraska Press, 2007); Scott Bowden and Bill Ward, *Last Chance for Victory* (Cambridge, MA: Da Capo Press, 2001); and Tom Carhart, *Lost Triumph* (New York: Penguin Group, 2005).

CHAPTER 7

1. John Wesley Powell, "Through the Grand," in *Liquid Locomotive*, ed. John Long (Helena, MT: Falcon Publishing, 1999).

2. Robert Kegan and Lisa Laskow Lahey, *How We Talk Can Change the Way We Work* (San Francisco: Jossey-Bass, 2001); Stephen Young, *Micromessaging* (New York: McGraw-Hill, 2007).

3. Robert D. Hoff, "Your Undivided Attention Please," *BusinessWeek*, January 19, 2004, 15.

4. Read, for instance, Robert E. Kelley, "In Praise of Followers," *Harvard Business Review*, November-December 1988. Review what followers can do to help leaders to succeed, Michael Useem, *Leading Up: How to Lead So You Both Win* (New York: Crown, 2001); Ira Chaleff, *The Courageous Follower: Standing Up To and For Our Leaders* (San Francisco: Berrett-Koehler, 1995).

5. Viktor E. Frankl, *Man's Search for Meaning* (Boston: Beacon Press, 2006) (originally published 1959), 139.

6. About.com: Twentieth Century History, "Alfred Nobel," http://history1900s.about.com/library/weekly/aa042000a.htm; Citizendium, "Alfred Nobel," http://en.citizendium.org/wiki/Alfred_Nobel.

CHAPTER 8

1. Craig Reynolds, "Boids: Background and Update," http://www.red3d.com/cwr/boids/.

2. Robert Keidel, *Game Plans & Corporate Players* (New York: E. P. Dutton, 1985).

3. Viktor E. Frankl. *Man's Search for Meaning* (Boston: Beacon Press, 2006) (originally published 1959), 154.

4. Philip Zimbardo, *The Lucifer Effect: Understanding How Good People Turn Evil* (Random House, 2007), 451–456

CHAPTER 9

1. Michael Useem, *The Leadership Moment* (New York: Three Rivers Press, 1998), Chapter 2.

2. Daniel Goleman, Richard Boyatzis, and Annie McKee, *Primal Leadership* (Boston: Harvard Business Press, 2002), 51.

3. Michael Useem. "Kenneth Chenault | Corporate Executive: The Ultimate Trial by Fire." *U.S. News and World Report*, November 12, 2007, 70. http://www.usnews.com/articles/news/best-leaders/2007/11/12/kenneth-chenault.html

4. Thomas Boswell, "The Best Manager There Is," *How Life Imitates the World Series*, 150-157.

5. Thinkexist.com, "Nelson Mandela Quotes," http://thinkexist.com/quotes/nelson_mandela/.

6. Jim Collins, *Good to Great* (New York: Harper Business, 2001).

7. Goleman, Boyatzis, and McKee, *Primal Leadership*, 52.

8. Thomas Boswell, "The Best Manager There Is," *How Life Imitates the World Series*, 150-157.

CONCLUSION, WHAT CONCLUSION?

1. Karl Fisch, "Did You Know?" http://thefischbowl.blogspot.com/2006/08/did-you-know.html.

2. "Though Upbeat on the Economy, People Still Fear for Their Jobs." *The New York Times*, December 29, 1996. http://www.nytimes.com/specials/downsize/1229econ-jobs-uncertain.html

3. Bradley Johnson, "Employment Numbers are Soaring, But so are Fears of Being Jobless," *Advertising Age*, Midwest Regional Edition 77, no. 8, (February 20, ,2006), 20. He draws on ISR annual survey.

4. Mihaly Csikszentmihalyi, *Flow: The Classic Work on How to Achieve Happiness.* (New York: Random House, 1992).

Index

Your Job Survival Guide orients you to our era of non-stop, accelerating change and offers you the skills necessary to thrive in this environment.

Other books focus on the broad, abstract principles of leading or surviving change. This book recognizes that your real job today is change and helps you get that job done in a crazy world...without driving yourself insane. You'll learn about pacing yourself...failing gracefully and recovering quickly...retaining optimism, resilience, and playfulness...protecting your career...leading loosely linked, ad hoc teams...setting your own course... prospering in an environment that demands more than ever, and can deliver non-stop adventure in return.

Leverage the power of play
Bring optimism and resilience to your workplace and your life

Learn to pace yourself, no matter what
Create "not to do" lists, take breaks, and be *in* but not *of* the chaos

Build a "personal flotation device" for your career
Develop the mindset and skills to recover from any setback

Communicate above the roar
Act with clear behavior, clear symbolic actions, and clear lines of sight

Lead and participate in ad hoc teams
Enhance your ability to make temporary teams succeed

Gregory Shea, Ph.D. consults, researches, writes, and teaches in the areas of organizational and individual change, leadership, group effectiveness, and conflict resolution. He is a Principal in The Coxe Group international consultancy; Senior Consultant at the Center for Applied Research; Adjunct Professor of Management at the Wharton School, where he has earned an Excellence in Teaching Award; and a Faculty Associate of the Wharton School's Center for Leadership and Change Management. A Phi Beta Kappa graduate of Harvard, Shea holds an M.Sc. from the London School of Economics and an M.A., M. Phil., and Ph.D. in Administrative Science from Yale. He is a member of the Academy of Management and the American Psychological Association.

Robert Gunther is coauthor or collaborator on more than 20 business books, including *The Truth About Making Decisions* and *The Wealthy 100*. He has consulted on communications for Fortune 500 companies and major non-profits. He has appeared on CNBC's "Power Lunch" and NPR's "Morning Edition," and his projects have been featured in the *New York Times, Time, USA Today,* and *Fortune*. His columns or articles also have been published in *Harvard Business Review, American Heritage,* and *Investor's Business Daily*. He is a graduate of Princeton University.